Constant

Awakening

Constant Awakening

SEARCHING FOR AND FINDING SPIRIT

A REMARKABLE TRUE STORY

HELENA STEINER-HORNSTEYN

ACTIVALE BOOKS

ACTIVALE BOOKS
P.O. Box 315
Sarasota, FL 34270
Email: activale@gmail.com
Website: www.activale.com

ISBN 978-0-9965689-0-6

Library of Congress Control Number: In Application

Printed in the United States of America

Cover art by Helena Steiner-Hornsteyn
Book design by Margaret Copeland/Terragrafix.com

"We don't know

the true nature of Reality

or what is truly Reality.

Because we compare

with our own limitations."

—Immanuel Kant
German Philosopher
1724-1804

This is my own Story of how I finally found Spirit,
And came to understand *why* we are here
And what is the Meaning of our Lives
—my life in particular.

To maintain privacy ALL names
have been changed

Contents

Foreword

I t takes great courage to live the life you want to live, rather than the one other people would like you to live. People thrive on the acceptance of others, often to their detriment. Helena Steiner-Hornsteyn embodies such courage, and chose self-acceptance over the lifestyle she'd been raised to embrace, when she turned, instead, to a calling that came from her heart and spirit.

Helena Steiner-Hornsteyn writes of the compelling, and often life-saving, experiences that not only cemented her acceptance of her gift, but showed her how to recognize and use spiritual knowledge and teach others to, as well.

How the spiritual affects the physical is a topic that has intrigued everyone, including scientists, for thousands of years. During the last decade of the 20th century, researchers finally began to gather proof in their scientific endeavors, publishing findings that clearly support that link.

Extraordinary experiences like Helena Steiner-Hornsteyn's can be studied for their clues to the true nature of coincidence, synchronicity and the power of spirit. Her book will make you question everything you think you know about yourself and the world around you—both seen and unseen. It's a story that was meant to be shared, and you will be moved by the woman who lived it.

— *Nina L. Diamond*
Miami, Florida

Nina L. Diamond is the author of *Voices of Truth: Conversations with Scientists, Thinkers & Healers.*

Author's Note

Constant Awakening has been written in response to the many queries I come across daily in my ministerial work as spiritual intermediary and medical intuitive. Every day I hear the questions: Why was I born to be the one I am? What is the purpose of my life? Is there a God? What is God? What about religion? What is the White Light? What happens when we die? Have I lived a previous life? What is intuition? Why do things always repeat themselves in life? How do I make good things happen in my life? Was my marriage really a mistake? How can I be happy? How will I stay well? And much, much more. The curiosity never ends.

I have found that the answers my clients listened to the most, were about how I, myself, discovered the way to higher knowledge and how I eventually found that inner peace that we all have been looking for. My clients also asked what advice I could give them, from my own experience.

The experiences I am going to share with you have been part of a long and incredible journey. As usual when you find yourself on a journey of discovery, trying to live it wasn't always that fun or easy. But then much later, when you have overcome your obstacles, you realize how much more knowledge you were able to add to your life through the process. You may even be grateful for the so-called bad times! And you may also recognize . . .Yes, there ARE such things as miracles!

True, the way I began my life may have been different from most since I was born with the gift to see through the dimensions, not only through the physical body, or the "mind": I was able to see energy-fields within and around people and find the cause behind why something was a certain way. At times I could also have conversations with those "on the other side."

I had no idea this was a gift. Instead I thought everyone could do the same, you just didn't talk about it. I also thought it was quite bothersome, and therefore made constant efforts to detach myself from my gift, a process in which for years I managed to blind-fold myself from the truth of who I really was.

We all do this. We all have the same wonderful connection to Spirit. Our true reality is much more extensive than we have ever been able to imagine. We are all shining Lights on Earth with unlimited possibilities within us.

Unfortunately, since birth we have been taught and conditioned to limit ourselves, to believe a certain way that leads us to look far away in the distance for help and support, when, ironically, the whole truth about ourselves can be found right here—within us.

Don't be mislead by the simplicity of this book. As you'll find, spiritual truth is simple, and the fact that we are spiritual beings in a physical body is easy and straightforward, but our intellect has made the uncomplicated Truth so very complicated. We have been made to believe that something so wonderful simply has to be full of twists and turns. But, this is not so. And, even better: Spirit is for absolutely every-one. Again, all we have to show is an open mind.

Constant Awakening is my own love story with Life, where, in the end we discover that each person or event in our existence was there for a purpose, and that they were predetermined to be in our lives to help us on our way to self-discovery.

Please, read the book carefully. Don't skip any pages. *Constant Awakening* is multidimensional. The more you read it, the more you will discover and learn. Each time it will seem like you are reading a new book. And in the end, you WILL understand the eternal meaning of I AM.

—*Helena Steiner-Hornsteyn D.D.*

Prologue

When I wrote the first edition of *Constant Awakening* more than a decade ago, times were more conservative and I was uncertain how far I should go in sharing my journey of how I found Spirit. My concern proved to be well founded: Once the book was out on the market, the established religious community had trouble understanding why I, an everyday woman and a religiously uninvolved Lutheran with no spiritual ambitions, had been chosen for experiences more suitable to biblical times.

The first published edition of *Constant Awakening* was the final result of an earlier attempt to write a book. I had spent one whole year of my life writing my story, eventually ending up with an almost 400-page long meticulously crafted manuscript. A publisher friend had offered early on to publish my work, and I believed I had it made.

At the time that I had finished writing the book, there was suddenly a buyer for my house, which had been on the market for almost a year. Consequently, on the spur of the moment, I had to drop all I was doing and begin packing.

To make sure I wouldn't lose any information stored on my computer, I made several spiral bound printed copies of my manuscript and carefully packed them in a well marked box, along with some of my favorite books. I also saved all notes and finished chapters on several floppy discs (which was the method we used in those days). I felt that I needed some extra time to edit and verify my material before I sent it off to the publisher.

However, through the most extraordinary circumstances, the movers dropped my computer on a tile floor. Not only did they break the computer, all of its memory was gone—and so was my story. I didn't worry too much at the time, however, as I still had the manuscripts saved on the floppy discs. But when I got a new computer, those discs had to be converted to new discs to suit the new computer model. So I asked my computer whiz to convert them onto a more modern version of storage discs. I waited and waited for him to return the discs, and when he eventually called me—he confessed that he had lost my floppy discs and thought he must have thrown them away by mistake, with some other old discs. I was shocked and speechless for a few days, but still hopeful because I knew I still had several printed copies somewhere in my boxes. It would of course mean extra work to convert them back to a computer file, but I took it in stride.

The next day I began to look for the special box with the manuscripts. I must have gone through every inch of my new home, but the box with the manuscripts was nowhere to be found.

It became clear that my manuscript and the year of life I had spent writing it were gone forever. I didn't even have one line left—all my creative ideas, all original chapters and drafts that had been saved on the computer hard drive, on discs and in print were lost.

Stunned, I eventually pulled myself together. At first, I was very disappointed with the whole Universe, wondering why this had happened to me. But I soon came to the realization that at least I had spent time with something I loved doing—soul searching and writing. In my mind, I convinced myself of all the benefits I had gained through my writing. It was true: I had found clarity in my relationship with Spirit and come to understand the meaning of life in general and my life in particular. I had come to accept that there is a meaning in everybody's life and that no one was born in vain.

What I had believed were mysteries before were mysteries no longer. In fact, I believed I had found the answers to many of my questions—why my life had happened the way it did, even why my book manuscript was gone. Without my year of soul searching, and all the channeled information given me in the process, I would most likely never have come to several of the deep insights I feel I have today. I had gone through a school of self-knowledge, making me more confident of Spirit and the work Spirit had planned for me. Writing a book had been the perfect way to find out who I was and why I was here.

A few years later I was asked by an agent why I didn't

have a book for my upcoming lecture tour—as everyone else did. Encouraged by a friend not to write such a long and detailed book, but instead to communicate with the public in an easily understood and shorter format, I began writing and with the help of Spirit channeled a new version of *Constant Awakening*. It was done in less than 2 months—focusing on my own experience and how I found the inner peace I had been looking for in my life. *Constant Awakening* was born.

Unfortunately, the publishing company that had committed to publishing the book earlier was now out of business, so I had to find another way to bring the message out in the open. Again through remarkable circumstances, the first edition of *Constant Awakening* was soon in print, in time for my lecture tour. (Not long afterwards, there was a second and third edition.)

For me it was a much needed good start and a message that no work is ever wasted, no matter what it is— you still always learn something new.

Rev. Dr. Helena Steiner-Hornsteyn
Sarasota, Florida
2015

Within you, there is a place

That knows all and sees all.

This is your Higher Potential

Your Higher Self

Your inner Light.

We set in motion that sparkle of Light within you

so you can be what Spirit intended you to be:

Happy, healthy and successful.

1

Encounter with the Burning Bush

There is a place of truth within each one of us, a place that knows all and sees all. This is our Inner Light, the God flame that shines within each one of us. This was the place that Spirit, patiently and time after time, wanted to awaken within me. Unfortunately, I was a very slow learner...

I am going to tell you a real-life saga. The story is my own adventure, and it took me many long years before I got the courage to share it with anyone else. It is my personal account of how I met the Light and how I eventually realized it was the ultimate truth. At the time it was the greatest meeting of my life, a one–on–one encounter with something I had to experience on my own. It would have been too hard to understand any other way. The memory of this experience still lives within me, day after day, year after year. It changed my whole outlook on life and opened the door to a new direction for my future. In fact, it not only changed my life, it brought peace to my heart. I believe it healed my life for all lifetimes to come.

My story begins one cold winter night in the beautiful old city of Lausanne in Switzerland, an elegant, historic city in the French-speaking part of the country. I was a young and self–involved teenager and had no idea about anything, except for what I experienced around me in my daily life of studies, gossip and general living of each day at a time. For a teenager of my background at that time in history, this was all you needed to know. I, of course, believed it to be everything.

This particular night, I was asleep in my student dorm, all alone in my little bedroom. It was a simple room with a narrow twin bed in one corner next to a nightstand with a lamp, a big writing desk in the center of the room with a simple wooden chair used for my studies, all lit up by a ceiling lamp on a long cord. There was also a dresser, a couple of chairs and an armoire. As a student, this was all I needed.

I had gone to bed as usual early in the evening, making sure the alarm was set for seven the next morning to have enough time to go through my daily routines before going to classes. Nothing had been different in any way on this chilly mid–winter night in the old, thick–walled residential building on the shores of Lake Geneva right in the heart of the European continent.

I was a fun–loving, nice–looking girl of 18, who had recently graduated from high school in Stockholm, Sweden. Full of expectations for my future, I was now going to a fashionable French-speaking preparatory school, as my first step into the world of international education. I had planned to later continue my studies at other European universities, to eventually make a career in the diplomatic service and fulfill a longstanding family tradition of living abroad.

"For the good of the world," I told others with a smile, knowing very well that my main reason at that time had more to do with the romance of the profession than a calling to help solve the world's many conflicts. At this time of my life, unquestionably I had only one thing in my mind: To enjoy life to its fullest and to see as much as possible of my big planet Earth. I had no spiritual ambitions whatsoever. At that time I didn't even believe in God and had never thought of God as being the Light—which is why what came to happen was even more surprising. No wonder my life would never be quite the same ever again...

All of a sudden, my heavy sleep was interrupted and I was wide awake. I can still remember how I was lying in bed, on my left side, staring into the darkness, and how I sensed an incredible presence behind me somewhere in my room. I felt a trembling, peculiar sensation flow through my body and I heard an almost hissing, crackling sound. Like electricity or fire. I hardly dared breathe.

"Oh my God, there's someone in my room." I was terrified at the thought of having an intruder in my bedroom, and my heart beat heavily as I wondered what to do. Then slowly, while holding my breath, I turned around, not knowing what on earth I would discover, or if someone was waiting for me behind my back.

Startled, and with my mouth open in disbelief, I saw something that seemed to look like a "sparkling fire" right in the center of my room. But, immediately, I realized: This was not a fire the way a fire was supposed to be. There was no heat, no smoke, and the flames were not yellow, but more like white, pale purple, and blue and they were full of little sizzling sparks. And it was . . . so incredibly alive! It almost resembled a Christmas tree on fire. Or to be more precise, it looked like a "burning bush" of sparkling energy right there amidst the furniture in the middle of my bedroom.

At first, my human logic tried to tell me that my new battery-operated radio standing on the table in the center of the room could have caught on fire. But, at the same time, I knew that a turned off battery radio could not possibly burn, and certainly not with these unusual, and big flames. I couldn't figure out what was going on, and realized that I was confronting something that was well beyond my comprehension.

I couldn't take my eyes off this "burning bush." Not knowing if minutes or seconds had passed by, I was frozen in time, absolutely amazed. And then, suddenly, I heard . . . "The Voice." A voice so powerful it can only be described as "unbelievable." To my amazement the voice spoke directly out of the burning bush and I had no doubt: It spoke directly to me! But I had no idea what the voice said. I refused to listen, and covered my ears with my hands the way I did as a small child, when I didn't want to listen to grown-up directions.

An unexplainable sparkling fire that wasn't really a fire, in the middle of my bedroom, and an undefined voice speaking out of flames that weren't really flames. This was too much to handle for an eighteen-year-old "jeune-fille," still untouched by life's many quandaries, and who was not yet used to facing anything outside the security of her own surroundings. I felt absolute terror, as I realized I was all alone facing this incredible mystery. I wanted nothing more than to get away from it all.

"Get me out of here," I wanted to scream. I wished I could run through the wall behind me to escape from this *whatever-it-was-presence* that was trying to besiege me. I felt confused, because although I was terrified, there was something familiar about both the fire and the voice: A recognition that touched me deep down in my soul, although I had no idea what it could be. It also appeared as if this mysterious something, in an odd way, was trying to enter into a place in my being, where I had absolutely no wish to be disturbed.

Whatever this sparkling, unnamed, and unspecified presence could be, I did not want to find out. All I knew was that I was not ready for it. Not now. Not yet. Maybe not ever. Because at this time in my life I was proud to belong to the carefree world of limitation I had learned to depend on, fully trusting that all my plans and wishes for a bright and beautiful life would easily come true as long as I did my best to fit in to the kind of life where I already played a role.

∽

I had no idea how wrong I was going to be.

Terrified, trying to avoid the intense light, and refusing to listen to what the voice had to tell me, I crawled deep down into my bed, covered myself with blankets and pillows, and decided that this bizarre presence simply had to go away. I didn't want any part of it!

"Please, please, leave me alone," I tried to scream out loud, but again, not a sound escaped my lips. "I don't want to, I don't want to . . ." I repeatedly thought. What I didn't want to hear or what I didn't want to do—I had no idea.

With that, I fell asleep, totally exhausted.

During the days that followed, I spent hours alone in my bedroom, looking for clues about what had happened during that special night of the "burning bush." There were no burn marks to show traces from a fire, no crossed wires, no disarrayed pieces of furniture, except for a glass of water that I had knocked over on my bedside table when I tried to get away from the intense presence of the burning bush. But worst of all, there was no one I could talk to about what could have happened, no one to ask what this was. I felt awful and very confused for a long time.

So I decided to forget.

But I didn't forget.

Instead, my life slowly began to change. Sometimes in a very subtle way, other times very dramatically. Always as if something unseen had interfered and pushed me into a new direction, I hadn't asked for or even wanted. This new path was very different from the one I had chosen for myself, almost as if there was another plan already made for me. And I was supposed to follow this plan, even if I seldom did. Sometimes it was so obvious, I had to laugh. Other times, it was extremely frustrating, because although I believed I made the right choices, often things just weren't going my way, no matter how hard I tried.

Many times, I would secretly visit what I considered sacred places, like a historic ruin, or beautiful places out in nature, where I would sit down and sense the peace of the souls who once lived there. Or I would go to a chapel or church, and inspired by the scent of burning candles and incense, say a prayer and walk out again. At the time, I couldn't understand why those visits were so important to me. Now, years later, I realize I was on the look-out for *something more*. But what should I call this *something more?* I did not know. At times, I experienced this feeling so intensely, it was as though if I found it, it would become part of me. Sometimes, I felt it was pulsating in my chest. Again, I didn't understand what this was, only that "this something" had to be an undefined Truth living within me. In my heart, I knew that it had to be the key to explaining the meaning of my life.

When my studies were completed and I was ready to begin my professional career—aiming at becoming a highly qualified diplomat for my country—I worked hard, but still enjoyed the glamorous side of life and felt privileged to be part of it. My life was extraordinary: I said yes to everything new, and hardly gave myself time to sleep in order to live life to its fullest. It seemed important to me to receive invitations to all the parties of the rich and famous, and to mingle with whom I believed at the time were the right people. I thoroughly enjoyed the famed, illustrious, and powerful, and I was proud that I could call many of them my good friends.

From time to time, I thought back to my early childhood when I was a little girl growing up in Sweden. As a child I was very talkative, outgoing and regarded quite "cute," like many other children. But I wasn't really like other children at all.

Even as a young girl, I had the ability to "turn on" a mental switch in my brain, and suddenly perceive energy fields in and around myself and others. In those energy fields I discovered various images: sometimes of deceased family members and other things I didn't understand. I was not always sure what those visions represented and why they were there. I didn't even know they were visions. How could I? I was just a child.

Grandmother understood who I was, because according to legend, through centuries, on my mother's side of the family, the occasional baby girl had been born with extraordinary sensitive abilities. Females who had grown up to be known for their wisdom, their connection to nature and extensive spiritual skills. Grandmother had told me that I had been given that same gift, but not once did she explain to me what this really meant, so I remained ignorant of the amplitude of my legacy. I had no idea that I could see what others could not see. I thought everyone was born with a kind of see-through, x-ray vision and that it was normal for everyone to look through each other's bodies, to perceive energy fields around us and to speak with loved ones now in spirit.

Of course, I had never heard of x-ray vision, spiritual experiences, energy-fields, dimensions or other fancy words at that time. This is what I have learned to call it now.

Not only could I see the energy-fields others knew nothing about. I could also "perceive" several layers of dimensions inside the human body. Almost like a blueprint of a building, with all the details of the hidden plumbing and wiring.

Again, I was so young and I couldn't understand what I saw and I didn't know what to call it. In the beginning, I took for granted that everyone could see the same things I did. But I was convinced it had to be very bad manners to talk about it, since I never heard anyone else ever bring it up. Actually, the ability to see through and around people rather bothered me, so often I did my best to push my visions away.

Early on, I came to the conclusion that what we call "dead," isn't really dead at all. On many occasions, while I was playing or just walking in the fields, I would perceive the presence of someone I knew was already dead, and they would tell me little messages.

"Tell them I am all right," a blond woman once said. She was so pretty. But I didn't know who she was, nor whom I could tell. She disappeared as quickly as she had appeared, and I wished I could have helped. But again, I didn't want to tell anyone about my meetings with the dead because nobody else ever spoke of such things.

I was always surprised that everyone "from the other side" was so happy. They always looked so youthful and relaxed, and always told me how great things were. A neighbor, whom I had known in life as white-haired and rather heavy, was "on the other side" slender with a tiny waist. Her hair was long and hazelnut brown, and she was full of joy.

"Finally, I can dance," she laughed, clapped her hands and danced around in an old-fashioned Swedish polka. "Nobody had time to dance with me before." And she told me to tell her family about a contract in a property deal that had never been signed, and that it needed to be taken care of.

Once I told a teacher I thought I could trust about my visions and she just laughed at me.

"You are mistaken," she said. "Only prophets in the bible can see things like that!"

From then on I never told anyone about my spiritual experiences. "Maybe I am mistaken," I would tell myself. My teacher had said I was, and I had always believed my school teacher knew everything. So I began to reject my visions and ignore the words I had previously heard from the beyond. Gradually, I stopped believing in what had been so much a part of my life. And as the years went by and I grew older, I had detached myself from my legacy since there seemed to be no place for it in my life. Soon I began to live the same carefree life as my peers—maybe even more so. And all those wonderful things I had learned to see around me and that had been so much a part of my life during my childhood, began to fade away and eventually disappeared out of my life.

Slowly I became like everyone else around me, seeing only things I was supposed to see and trusting only what everyone could touch or notice. It appeared easier that way. And I considered myself reasonably happy until that dark winter night in Switzerland when the Light came to pay me a visit—this time in the shape of the Burning Bush . . .

Through the years, at the oddest times I found myself reliving the meeting with the Burning Bush. I could still hear that powerful Voice ringing through my ears, and I tried, in vain, to figure out what it wanted me to know.

Why was it so hard to remember?

Of course, I had been so unwilling to listen and had done all I could to escape.

What didn't I want to hear?

What had the Voice tried to tell me?

What was the Burning Bush?

Why did it come to see me?

Yes, why me?

Many years would have to pass and I would have to go through countless mistakes, much learning, and a series of several spiritual awakenings before I would be able to understand the simple truth. Not until then did I finally understand the meaning of my meeting with the Burning Bush: It was a reminder that a human being is a spiritual being. A reminder that I (yes, me too) am a spiritual being. And the flaming bush was my connection.

It was my first wake-up call.

Unfortunately, I didn't know this at the time, so I did absolutely nothing about it. Instead, I gladly continued my glamorous and frivolous life, still looking for a clue about what it all meant.

But I didn't know, then, about the persistence and determination of Spirit: Apparently a plan had been made for me long before I was born. Although I had been given the *free will* to follow this plan in this lifetime or not, the plan was still going to present itself to me, again and again, until I was willing to go along with it. And when I finally went along with the plan, I was also to discover that I had been given a gift, a special link to the Universe and that this connection in no way could be treated with disrespect.

It would take many long years to understand the work of Spirit: To be worthy of a privileged connection to the Universe, I, like everyone else on this Earth, had to walk a particular route. Not always an easy one, because what could you learn and what wisdom could you acquire if everything always goes your way?

But at the same time, I have been given the freedom to use my free will as much and as often as I wish. Because of the choices I would make, I would feel doubt from time to time, sometimes very deep in my human mind, and it had to be cleared away before a new level of knowledge would open up before me. And with that awakening, I would not only be able to see more, understand more and have a greater vision, I would also have reached one level further on my road of spiritual maturity.

Eventually, I would arrive at the level where I'd be able to say: Yes, I DO believe. Yes, I truly do. And my eyes would see what I didn't see before, and my ears would hear what I couldn't—or wouldn't—hear before.

Looking back at the moment of my first awakening, I have now learned to understand that we have to continue opening doors in order to reach the ultimate Truth. Not just one door that we call our end station of knowledge, even if we feel so at the time, but one door after the other.

Because the Truth is never ending.

2

Never Alone

There was no question in my mind that somewhere close by, some kind of Higher Intelligence was watching out for me. I thought of this Higher Intelligence as a Master Energy and had accepted that I didn't know much about it. Only that "IT" seemed to be well aware of what was going on in my life, no matter where I was, and that "IT" had even cared to step in and save my life when no other options were left. Although I could find no logical proof for this, there was no other explanation for why things had happened the way they did. I really wasn't sure where this Master Energy was located or how to reach it. I only knew that it definitely existed, and that it had shown me that it wanted to take me to a level of "my highest good."

I was certain that I'd been saved by an unexplainable Higher Power, when, as a young college student, I had decided to drive my little sports car back to Geneva in the far west corner of Switzerland from London, where I'd been visiting friends for a few days. I had cut my stay short and was now eager to get back to Switzerland to celebrate Christmas with a special friend.

While in England, I hadn't kept up with the news in France or in Switzerland, so I had no idea that a terrible snowstorm had been forecast for the mountainous part of eastern France, and that a travel advisory had warned people to stay off the roads.

Toward the end of the day, as I approached the Alps, after a rather smooth drive through the French countryside, it was already snowing so hard that I couldn't see the road signs. But believing I knew the route well, I continued and it was not until much later, after I found myself on a narrow and very slippery serpentine road in a deserted part of the French Alps, that I realized my mistake and understood I was lost. Desperately, I tried to find my way back through the deep snow to a safer road, but eventually I got stuck in the middle of the winding road as heaps of deep snow quickly piled up around my stranded little car. Shocked to find the gas gauge on empty, I immediately knew that I was helplessly on my own, because I'd already realized that I'd ended up on a road that was closed for the winter season. And I also knew that several months would pass before anyone would travel that road again. To make it worse, nobody in the whole world had any idea where I was, because I'd left London a couple of days early to surprise my special friend in Switzerland.

I was now in a place of no return and I had accepted that there was absolutely nothing I could do—but slowly freeze to death.

"But I'm not ready to die yet," I suddenly cried out in total despair as the darkness of the night began to fall. I was shivering with cold and fear. I was hungry, and thirsty, and I was in no way dressed for the heavy winter weather outside the car. I felt tremendously sorry for myself and knew that, short of a miracle, I had no way out.

And then I remembered Spirit.

"Listen," I called out in the cold air. "I'll change, I'll do whatever you want me to do, if you'll help me live through this." I promised out loud that if I survived, there was one particular thing I was going to do. I was specific. But what this commitment was, I cannot reveal to the world, because it will forever remain between me and Spirit. Then I prayed like never before. And prayed some more, and I imagined how I was happily back home, enjoying a warm summer day with a clear blue sky and a few scattered white clouds. I was a happy little girl again, sitting in the middle of a field with my hands full of beautiful flowers . . . .

And all of a sudden—I had to rub my eyes to believe it—strong gusts of wind suddenly appeared from nowhere and blew the deep snow off the road. Miraculously, I had a clear passage in front of me!

Amazed, I turned the start key just once, shifted into gear, and the stalled car moved again! And then the heat came back on, and, as in a dream, I continued my drive through the night. After what seemed a lifetime, when I eventually saw the city lights of the Swiss city of Geneva appear deep down in the valley below me, I finally cried. I knew I'd been saved. But how the snow would blow away to open the road, and how the car could run on an apparently empty gas tank, I will never understand. I just thankfully accepted that this was so.

Although I was safely back home, I remembered to keep my promise to Spirit. I did not particularly like my promise, and it later proved to be a nuisance to keep it. But a promise is a promise. You keep a promise, no matter what, particularly if it is a commitment to Spirit. And I am convinced that this commitment not only gave me my life back, it also validated my connection to Spirit. Many times during the years to come, I found that a power higher than my own had unexpectedly moved in to help me out when times were tough.

I recall the season when I was completing my studies in Paris at a time when practically every day the city directly or indirectly experienced the political conflict between France and the French North African colony of Algeria. The Algerians were fighting for their independence from France and there were outbreaks of terrible violence both in France and North Africa. Little did I know that I, too, would get involved, after I had helped the French police identify a group of terrorists after they set off a bomb close to a famous street café in the St. Germain de Pres section of Paris. Shortly afterwards, angry Algerians retaliated and made one attempt after another on my life. Luckily, each time, I narrowly escaped. When one day a well-aimed bullet missed me by just a split second—only because I had made a totally unexpected move, I finally decided to leave Paris until the political turmoil was over. It would take over three years before I would visit Paris again.

And I remember vividly when I was driving in a mountainous area in Italy. As in a trance, suddenly and for no apparent reason, I pulled aside, and at that very moment an enormous truck swerved around the corner on my side of the road. Had I been there, my car would for sure have been pushed off the road and I would've crashed on the valley floor hundreds of feet below me. Not only would my life, as I had known it, have been over. But most of all, the life I was meant to live would never have begun.

Then there was the time when I was walking in full daylight in the bazaars of the streets of Tunis in North Africa, and a man pulled me into a side street with a knife to my face. In the scuffle that followed, our eyes suddenly met, and I looked him straight in the eye. At that moment my fear suddenly disappeared and I couldn't help smiling. Why, I will never understand. I don't know what he saw in my eyes, but he screamed, and immediately dropped me to the ground. He quickly disappeared without a trace.

I was saved.

As my awareness grew, I came to realize that many miracles had often touched my life. Unsure why and how this could have been possible, I could only give my thanks, absolutely convinced that Something or Somebody had indeed been watching out for me. I also understood that this kind of thing has happened and could happen to all of us at some time or the other. Unfortunately, most of us are just too afraid to speak out, uncertain what others would say, believing "those others" wouldn't understand what we are talking about.

3

Meeting with the Light

A long time had passed since my adventurous days as a young single woman. I was now married to Hans-Wilhelm, a tall, handsome, blue-eyed German, a man of solid education and several doctorates from both European and American universities, and with an impressive background of philosophical and religious knowledge. He was a much respected man with a large following in his particular field of knowledge. Hans-Wilhelm was my second husband.

My first husband, George, a jet-setting English nobleman, had been killed in a dramatic car accident on the French Riviera only two years earlier. George and I maintained several homes in different interesting places and we lived a dream of no worries. We often traveled from party to party from one country to the other, always first class with champagne in our hands. I was young, in love and believed I had made it. I lived on top of the world. And naturally, I took for granted that my good fortune would stay with me for the rest of my life.

After George's death, at first, I thought my life was over, but after some time and with much hurt, I pulled my shattered dreams together and with only two exclusive Bond Street leather suitcases in my hands, I started life all over again. I had been lucky: With all my good international connections I had immediately been offered a freelance position as a goodwill negotiator and was immediately sent to Eastern Europe, at that time called "the countries behind the Iron Curtain." With the Cold War going on between the western and eastern hemisphere, the tension was strong, and trust was hard to come by.

But I did well and was soon asked to preside at several international conferences, focusing on new commercial relations between the two blocks of power. As in a daze, I shook many hands and spoke to many more people, enjoying meeting each person as well as doing well with my work. Still in a state of shock from George's sudden death, I was unaware of my professional luck, and that I had gained a position previously unheard of for a woman of my age. After some time, I met Hans-Wilhelm, a meeting that was to change my life forever.

From the beginning Hans-Wilhelm and I had an amazing spiritual connection, as if we'd known each other since the beginning of time, and we married after just a few weeks of togetherness. We seemed to share the same open-minded philosophy and could talk for hours to satisfy our mutual thirst for more insight into the higher realms.

"Where did you learn all this?" he often wondered, when I inexplicably knew the answers to many of his spiritual issues. We were both baffled, because he was considered to be the expert and sometimes made appearances to that effect on radio or television shows. I, on the other hand, at that time had absolutely no divinity training. I was just a former jet-setter, used to a glamorous and expensive lifestyle and, according to the world, I wasn't supposed to know anything about Spirit and I certainly was not supposed to be capable of any deep philosophical thoughts.

But I soon realized, I had come home. After all, feminine spiritual wisdom was part of my heritage, and although I had not yet practiced in that field, where I could use my knowledge, I had always been proud to be a direct descendant of so many legendary wise women living for centuries before me. What I didn't know was that Hans-Wilhelm was to show me a side of life that I had never known before. A life where Spirit was a friend and a phenomenon of all dimensions, and available to all of us, not only a chosen few.

On this particular day, Hans-Wilhelm and I had been out for a hike in the mountains, and had returned to the quaint, little inn by the idyllic Lake Wolfgang in the Austrian Alps not far from Salzburg, near the German-Austrian border, where we were spending a few relaxing days. The day had been beautiful and we decided to share a jug of the local wine before dinner as we watched the golden sunset behind the awesome mountain peaks. The view was breathtaking.

Hans-Wilhelm and I went to bed early that night, tired after our long outing in the mountains. We had spoken about our future. After much traveling, we felt it was time to settle down and to start a family, and we made plans to build a new house in the beautiful Black Forest area of South Germany. I was content that I'd finally found a place and circumstances where I thought I belonged, and where I could be like other young women my age.

But then it happened again: After years of absence, "The Light" was calling me for a second meeting:

With no forewarning, I was suddenly awakened in the latter part of the night by an incredibly bright light in our bedroom. Not knowing what on earth was going on, I instantly sat up in bed, grabbing my pillow to protect myself against this unknown presence. There was so much light in the room, it was almost blinding, as gushes of light rolled toward me like ocean waves. As soon as one wave reached me, a new, much brighter wave appeared. At first, the absurd thought crossed my mind that strangers had intruded into our bedroom, and were looking at us with big flashing lights. But of course, that was not so.

Hans-Wilhelm was sleeping next to me in bed, but to my surprise he rolled over and turned his back, and didn't seem to be bothered by the strong waves of light. He kept on sleeping, and as he disappeared into deep darkness, the incredible waves of white light continued to roll toward me.

And then . . . I heard the Voice:

How well I remember that voice!

It was *THE* voice. The same voice I had encountered in my bedroom during that cold winter night in

Switzerland, emanating from what I will always call the Burning Bush and I remember how frightened I had been. This time the voice was much more powerful, speaking to me directly, and there was no way I could avoid listening to it, a feeling of submission too hard to explain in words. But this time I wasn't scared. On the contrary. I was willing to listen.

And the Voice spoke:

"Do not forget the first Commandment:
You shall have no other Gods before ME!"

Anyone who ever hears this voice will have no doubt that this is the Ultimate Truth. No words will ever describe the greatness of this experience.

"DO NOT FORGET THE FIRST COMMANDMENT:
YOU SHALL HAVE NO OTHER GODS BEFORE ME."

The words are still, today, ringing in my ears:

"You shall have no other Gods before ME."

"You shall have no other Gods before ME . . . ME . . . ME . . . ."

Not until years later did I understand the true meaning of humility. It simply means *to let go* and to listen to Spirit *without* human judgment and reasoning. To understand humility is to know that it is impossible to hear the Truth *directly* from Spirit when, or if, you have decided to remain in the state of human logic and indoctrination!

" . . . before ME . . . ME . . . ME . . . ."

The Voice's energy echoed through the air for a few moments, then it slowly faded away. But the waves of Light continued to roll toward me, each one delivering a new message. The messages were clear and to the point, and I made no judgment about why they were given to me. Instead, I showed a total openness to the moment, and as I did, I suddenly felt powerful beyond measure, as if I was part of the surrounding Light and the Light was part of me.

As I was now part of the Light, it was easy to understand each message that the bright rolling waves had delivered to me. No rational thoughts crossed my mind at the time, and it wasn't until afterwards that I discovered that each message expressed an answer to questions I'd never openly asked, but had deep down wanted to have answered.

"Who are you who speaks to me?" I wanted to know as one more wave of light rolled towards me.

"It's ME, Spirit.
I am the light that shines within you."

"But WHO are you?"

"I am....Your I AM.
I am the beginning and end of the one you are."

"But WHO are you?"

"I am the Creation of All That Is."

"But WHO?"

"*I AM what you are. I am your Higher Self.*"

"I don't understand?"

"*I AM . . . "ME" IN YOU!*
I AM the one you call Spirit.
I AM the Light within you.
I have given you your life."

"What do you mean by . . . Before ME?"

"*I AM*" *within you came FIRST, and will remain First.*
I know all, see all, hear all . . . .
You tune in with ME and you will find your
direction."

"But I haven't learned it that way."

"*So, learn again:*

I AM is "ME" within you,
Your Higher Self.
And I know all, see all, hear all . . ."

"I still don't understand!"

"I AM in you is your real life.
I AM is the Eternity within you.
I am the Light that shines within you.
I AM is the vehicle you use to fulfill your dreams."

"But I still don't understand . . . ."

"When you begin to let go, you WILL understand:
"I AM" is the Light within you that keeps you alive.
Your body will one day change and eventually disap-
pear, but your I AM never will.
"I AM" is the truth of the one you truly are.
Always.
"I AM" is everywhere.
Yes, also within each and everyone.
Particularly so.

I AM is a place within you, your soul-light.
That place that knows all, hears all, sees all . . . .
This is the truth of what and who you are.
Do you now understand?"

"Yes, I AM THE LIGHT is my soul-light and the energy of Spirit in me."

"Now, allow yourself to shine!
Honor your I AM,
Honor what you truly are!
I AM is the Truth and the Creator within you!
This is the First Commandment."

All of a sudden, a vision of planet Earth appeared before me in an outburst of light. People lived all over the planet, but in some places certain individuals shone with extraordinary brightness, almost like stars. I was told they were the "enlightened ones." And although they were distant from each other, they were all connected, and would always be able to find each other anywhere in the world.

Amazed, I looked at those individuals as their glow increased in strength. Soon their light was getting so strong that they began to rise higher and higher—way above planet Earth. And when they did, they joined hands around Earth—and soon turned into real stars.

Slowly, the waves of Light disappeared around me and soon the room was dark again. I wished the Light could have stayed a little longer, because it made me feel so good. Now, all I heard was the stillness of the night and my husband breathing beside me.

It was impossible to fall asleep again, and I waited until the first rays of the morning sun touched our bedroom window. Then I walked out into the crispness of the cool autumn morning for a walk up the mountains. I watched crows congregate in a tree and a deer family ran right by me. And I felt such a connection with them and the whole world. But I had to be alone for a while and digest my experience.

Could I tell anyone about my meeting with the Light?

I wasn't sure.

Then I remembered how one of the waves of light had told me to go out into the world to tell others. But tell whom? And tell them what? Hans-Wilhelm was the expert in the field. What would he say? Maybe I should've tried to wake him up. Would he be upset with me now? Slowly, I began to doubt that I would have the courage to tell the world, especially those who had not asked to be told. I had a good life. Why should I get involved and deliberately ask for trouble?

I wasn't even certain of the first commandment anymore. How did it read again? I thought I knew my ten commandments from the Bible's Old Testament. But, maybe I didn't. I was confused and felt I was facing an incredible choice: should I remain closed in among high walls or move ahead toward uncertainty? And I kept on wondering: "Why did this happen to ME?" Yes, why *me*?

There was no explanation.

So I never told anyone.

I wasn't ready yet, nor did I think the world was ready to listen to what I had to say.

But, now, decades later, the Light has reappeared and reminded me of my obligation. Finally, I am ready to let go! And I am very willing to tell the world.

Yes, I now know that within me there is a core of limitless knowledge. This incredible Energy is called I AM and is the Loving Presence of Spirit within each one of us.

And I also understand that this Energy is the true reality of my being, making me a spiritual being inside a physical body. The essence of this Energy is of a frequency so high that with the limitation of my human mind, I can only comprehend it as an extraordinary bright White Light.

This Higher Power within each one of us belongs to the Eternity and will one day go back to the Eternity after my human body's mission has been fulfilled.

It is that simple.

The waves had made me understand this principle on which all traditions and cultures had founded their belief systems. But, then, this principal idea had often been adjusted to conform with what was suitable for that homeland and particular culture or government. Once spirituality had come under human control and specifications, this was the time when religion was born.

From the day of my first awakening, when I had encountered the Burning Bush, I would often take a moment away from the crowd and secretly go to a place of worship, where I would light a candle and stay for a quiet prayer. I didn't understand why, because although I came from a Protestant background, and had been both baptized and confirmed into the Christian faith, I hadn't been religious, and places of worship had never meant anything to me before. During those times of stillness I developed a relationship with Spirit, and although I was still uncertain what it really was, of one thing I was absolutely certain: This Power was so much higher and more knowledgeable than I was.

I enjoyed those times when Spirit and I were together in a one-on-one relationship without anyone else interfering. It made me feel safe and good about myself. With time, I discovered I could be in any country, in any place and experience that same intimate bond with Spirit. Because, in truth, Spirit was everywhere. And, as I eventually found out through my own experience, I was part of Spirit, and Spirit was part of *me*, since, in truth, there is no separation.

Several days after my meeting with the Light at Lake Wolfgang, it suddenly occurred to me that when I looked at an individual a certain way, I could see all kinds of energy-waves around him or her in the same way I used to when I was a little girl. And I also realized that I could see "through" their bodies and detect organs, and also symbols for things I didn't yet understand, and I could "see" energies moving around inside their physical bodies, energies I knew didn't belong.

44

Intuitively, I understood those were blockages causing problems for them.

"But perhaps I have seen this all along?" I wondered, and remembered how as a child my whole world seemed to be filled with visions and impressions I couldn't understand, and how I'd considered them such a burden. Maybe those visions had been with me all along, but I'd refused to recognize them in my effort to grow up, and to be a regular human being. And then I'd been so busy, I simply must have forgotten I had a special gift.

But now the White Light had opened my eyes— and I could "see" again! Maybe even more so than ever before . . . .

I found that everything alive exuded its own energy-waves and that those waves could determine the condition of its well-being. And I also found an alignment of energy centers in people's physical body and I called those places "power stations." It was so exciting to discover that each one of these power stations would shine in a different color and exude energies of their own. When one of those power stations was closed and had lost its color, it could no longer send good healthy energy to the surrounding physical body and people would get sick. Sometimes I could see images in the energy-field around each individual, images that didn't belong there and needed to be removed, but nobody knew how to do so.

I found that since birth each individual had been provided with a detailed multidimensional blueprint of their whole physical and emotional system, inside out. And this blueprint also included memories of their past, going back to a time far beyond conception.

It had all come back to me . . .

This was my second awakening.

4

Love and Let Go

After meeting with the White Light at Lake Wolfgang in Austria, I finally understood that what happens in life can't always be just a coincidence. Instead, I was convinced that life is an avenue of constant awakenings and that one is supposed to go along with it—sooner or later. Although I didn't follow what Spirit had asked me to do at the time, I was soon made aware that something important must have happened through our meeting "in the Light."

Because not only did my "seeing" ability return, I also began to feel an urge to help those who were sick and unfortunate. The word soon spread of my spiritual abilities, although at that time, I did my best to hold them back in public. My eating habits also changed dramatically: I became very aware of what I was to eat and intuitively pushed away so many foods I considered not valid for human consumption.

After my experience with the Light at Lake Wolfgang, I had found that I could reconstruct some of the beneficial energy of the White Light at any time, and that through my intention, I could bring back its radiant energy and sweep it around me. And when I bathed in the bright light, it made me feel balanced and protected. I often met with the Light during my meditations and soon the Light had become my very intimate friend, always willing to strengthen me in times of need.

I had no reason to believe that anything was going to interfere with my happiness with Hans-Wilhelm. We sometimes talked about death and what we believed would happen to us after we died. Since both of our spouses had died unexpectedly in our previous marriages, we were now confident that we were deserving of a long, happy life together and we thought of death as something that would just happen to others. Only jokingly would we ever bring up what we would do, if one of us passed on before the other.

"If you go first," I told Hans-Wilhelm, "I'll insist you return to tell me all about it." And of course, I promised him I'd do the same. And we meant it. Naturally we were confident that first we would have a very long and happy life ahead of us.

But our life together was going to be cut very short. One cool spring evening close to our home in the beautiful old town of Baden-Baden in South Germany, Hans-Wilhelm died after a freak car accident. His death was instant and totally unexpected—but death usually is.

For weeks afterwards, I wondered what I could've done to prevent his death. I was filled with guilt and anger and reprimanded myself almost daily for not preventing him from leaving the house that fatal evening. It would've been so easy for me to ask him to stay: I was setting the table for a late, candlelight dinner in front of the fire, for just the two of us, when Hans-Wilhelm decided to go out for a short walk. He assured me he would be back in just a few minutes.

But he didn't come back, and I waited and waited, and when the telephone finally rang, I answered on the first ring. I thought he had stopped by at a neighbor's house, because he sometimes did. But a strange woman from the local hospital was on the line. I sat down and didn't understand at first. Who? Hans-Wilhelm? No, he was not at home. I didn't understand and had to ask again. What? He wasn't coming home? In a daze, I learned that Hans-Wilhelm was not coming home . . . ever.

A car had hit him as he was crossing the street only a few blocks away. Hans-Wilhelm never regained consciousness and died shortly afterwards at the hospital, where he had been taken by an ambulance. We never had the chance to say goodbye.

I couldn't understand. Why him? Why me? Why us? We'd made so many wonderful plans. There had to be a mistake. Of course there was a mistake. The hospital had made a mistake. They had the wrong man. Or maybe they had just dialed the wrong number. Of course, that was it: they had dialed the wrong number. They had never meant to call me at all. They wanted to reach someone else. They couldn't mean us; we had plans; we had a good life and we had only just begun . . . .

Or maybe this was only a dream, and I would soon wake up and find him sleeping by my side. I refused to understand. But the truth was eventually clear. Hans-Wilhelm was gone.

One more time in my young life, I was an instant widow. What on earth had I done wrong?

One night several weeks after Hans-Wilhelm's funeral, I was gently woken up in the middle of the night. No lamps were turned on in my bedroom, but a bright white light, apparently coming from nowhere, completely filled my bedroom. And suddenly, in front of my open eyes, there he was: Hans-Wilhelm, sitting in the center of our large bed. He was surrounded by an intense white light.

"But you are dead!" I burst out. I'll never forget how I almost accused him for having passed on and for leaving me alone. But he only smiled and took me in his arms. We embraced and held each other close, and when we did, it seemed as though I left my physical body behind and was absorbed into the Light. Because I now experienced a love and tenderness that were so far above any physical passion I had ever experienced before.

It was not until the following day that I understood how the White Light had created a place of unconditional Oneness for us: A world of total freedom, where we both could meet without any kinds of judgments. A place of no restriction where we were allowed to forget the worlds that each one of us represented, in an atmosphere where I could leave my physical body, tears, and suffering behind.

After our meeting in the Light, we could've parted forever and I would never have seen Hans-Wilhelm again. But it was impossible for me to say goodbye, I couldn't forget and I was not yet willing to let go. So I made it my choice to meet him again.

Night after night, Hans-Wilhelm returned for a visit and we would be together, embracing each other in the Light. Gradually, I began to drift into his world, forgetting I had to eat and drink and communicate with others during the day. I began to physically fade away, because I was now unable to maintain the balance between our two realms and had forgotten that I belonged to a world where one had to eat and drink to stay alive, pay electricity bills to see the light, use a vehicle to get places, and a telephone to communicate with the world. I had no idea that I had now stepped into the very dangerous level of playing with the dimensions and that I had begun to let go of the physical life where I still belonged.

One night, Hans-Wilhelm told me about his beautiful existence in a place he liked to call "the Land of Continuation," and that he loved being there.

"Come with me," he said.

But I hesitated. How much I wanted to stay with him into eternity, but . . . I shook my head:

"No, I'm not ready yet," I heard myself say. "There is so much I still want to do . . . ."

And suddenly I was convinced that I'd been given my own life as a gift and privilege, and that I had not yet given this life and myself the chance we deserved. There was still so much I hadn't tried. I wanted to have children, learn more, see more. I was particularly eager to learn the reason for my life on this Earth, and where I would play a part.

I was relieved when I told Hans-Wilhelm that I wouldn't go with him, and noticed that this was the answer he'd expected from me. In our final goodbye, I asked him never to visit me again. The time had come for both of us to move on. I would have to start my life all over again—yet one more time! Finally, I understood what it meant to love unconditionally: I loved him so much, I was willing to let him go.

I never saw Hans-Wilhelm again.

When I woke up the next morning, I was full of bouncing energy. I made telephone calls all over the country, planned an agenda and I was hungry, very hungry. Energized with a new will to live, I was ready to give my world a new start.

I had finally realized that Hans-Wilhelm's physical body, the one that I had touched and loved so much was forever gone. What I had met in my "dream" was his "Body of Light," and I understood that this was really "the body" I had loved all along. But I could never make any claims on his body of light, because our body of light can only belong to the Universe.

After I was willing to give Hans-Wilhelm back to the Universe my healing occurred almost instantly. I knew he and I would meet again, on our journey through eternity, when the energy of our light bodies, our souls, would cross paths again. And when our energies would meet, we would immediately know it, because our souls would instantly recognize each other.

It happens all the time.

5

The End Is a Good Beginning

I was admiring the futuristic Miami skyline from the aft deck of the yacht Ocean Goddess, a 108-foot dream of traditional yachting elegance, as we slowly approached the Florida coastline. A light south-eastern breeze filled with the salty essence of the ocean was sweeping across the open areas of the yacht, as the sun was setting behind the tall buildings of downtown Miami, sending a golden shimmer across the calming waters of Biscayne Bay. I could never get enough of Florida sunsets and filled with thankfulness for my good fortune, I comfortably sat down in a plush rattan armchair with my two little Pomeranian lap dogs in my arms. The scene was as beautiful as a picture cut from a glossy magazine and this picture was now what I called my life.

I was now married to Jack, a good-looking and shrewd American businessman who enjoyed good times, and although he possessed an almost extrasensory feeling about how to handle business matters, he was without any spiritual ambitions. The yacht was ours and we were on our way back to Miami after having entertained some of Jack's business associates for a short ocean cruise. Our teenage daughter, Annabel, was relaxing with her ever-chatting and laughing girlfriends somewhere on the top deck of the yacht. I enjoyed being a mother, a wife, and that there were no major worries in my life.

I now had the family I had so longed for, complete with the husband, the child and the pets. My hair was now glamorously long and blond, and I had learned to wear colorful clothes with matching custom jewelry. We were very much part of the fascinating South Florida social scene and were well-known for our lavish parties. In one way our life was a timeless

Never-Never Land and I must admit, I did have a very good time!

Jack had been introduced to me by a casual acquaintance only a year after Hans-Wilhelm's death, when I was in Florida to appear on a couple of television shows. I was to speak about my Institute for Positive Thinking that I had recently founded in West Berlin only a stone's throw away from the Berlin Wall, at that time separating the communist East Berlin from the allied sector of West Berlin. But when Jack and I met, I forgot all about my television shows, and all about my continued plans for my Institute. I even forgot that I had several thousand people who were waiting for me to return to Germany. Because when I looked into Jack's clear blue eyes, it felt like coming home, and I didn't want to go away ever again.

We married only two weeks after we met, in a big dazzling wedding aboard his spectacular private yacht. We were deeply in love, and I was convinced that Spirit had finally sent me a well-deserving reward of lasting happiness.

A few years of incredible bliss followed, but soon I found that what I believed was going to be an easy and carefree life was not going to be so easy after all. And the values I had brought with me from working with those who needed my help somehow didn't fit in to my new life so filled with social pleasures. So, yet one more time, I gradually pushed away the truth about myself and my connection to the Light, and denied the multidimensional ability of my seeing eyes.

Instead, I became the hostess with the biggest parties in the biggest house, always surrounded by a large circle of friends, forgetting there was a much bigger world beyond the one where I lived. Quickly, one year was added to the next. The years turned into decades. I was still laughing and dancing, but one day I woke up and was surprised how fast a life can slip by.

"Is this all there is?" I suddenly asked myself as I had ended yet another year of play, and began to question the meaning of my life. This couldn't have been what I was meant to do in life. I knew it, because all along I had sensed there was something else so close by, but for some reason I was unable to reach it. I could just as well have walked barefoot through the world looking for a place to sleep. And I knew that if I lived through another year of my life, it would not make much difference to what I already was experiencing. And although I wasn't sure why, I felt I was wasting my time.

In search for that something "more," I left Florida for the Scandinavian wilderness to visit my family estate in Warmland in west Sweden, a province well known for its almost mysterious beauty, and for being the homeland of so many famous authors and artists. But I was still not satisfied, and not knowing what I was looking for I left the comfort of the big house and decided to spend some time alone in one of our cabins by the Lake Var, far out in the wilderness. It was refreshing to leave the world's noises behind, and as I experienced nature in the revealing light of the midnight sun, I began to hear the unheard. I found that there was no such thing as stillness. Not at all. Because in the depth of the stillness we may hear the biggest sounds. And out of this stillness, so generously offered to me by nature, I slowly began to realize that through those many years of hectic socializing, I had lost the foundation of what I was all about.

And then nature spoke to me about the depth of "All." About coming from somewhere and about going to a particular place. About the Power that kept it all together. And about belonging. To belong I had to "tune in." But tune in to what?

Sadly, I recognized I'd been tuned in to a station that was never mine.

Through the many years of my marriage to Jack, I had forgotten the message given to me at Lake Wolfgang. It wasn't Jack's fault. On the contrary, nobody was to blame but me, because I had to admit only I alone could be responsible for my choices. Naturally, I had never told Jack about my experience at Lake Wolfgang, when Spirit so dramatically had shown me the meaning of the Light. But instead of being faithful to the knowledge, as soon as I married, I pushed the Light away, and replaced it with a whirl of dingle-dangle values that I had believed were more important at the time. And in the process, I was slowly losing the connection to my true Self.

Why had I replaced the message of Lake Wolfgang with the values of materialism? It wasn't necessary to take sides. I could have stayed with the Light and still enjoyed the good pleasures of the world. Didn't I know that affluence could also be a sign of spiritual success and not necessarily the opposite of the Divine?

And what had happened to TIME? It had gone by so fast. Where were the visions I used to have? And what had happened to my healing hands?

To the world, I had kept on smiling. I had done well. I had even founded my own charity organization in Florida and was constantly raising funds for those in need. I also produced concerts with famous stars, where all proceeds would go to the needy, and I enjoyed my star-studded entertaining events, my friends and being in demand. My life was exciting, but within me I was slowly going through a deep crisis. I had lost my intimate friendship with my Light!

Over the years, the happiness that Jack and I once had became overshadowed by envy and many intrigues, and as a result, our marriage was slowly falling apart. After a long and intense marriage, the inevitable happened, and we ended up in a very lengthy and troublesome divorce. I was devastated and blamed myself for having failed, because when we married, I truly believed our marriage was meant to last forever.

But, with time, I understood that what I'd considered to be a failure in fact had turned out to be the best lesson of my life. And the feeling of defeat that had burdened me was eventually replaced by an incredible feeling of gratitude to Spirit for giving me the opportunity to learn something that I obviously needed to learn. My lesson was to experience first hand that self-healing depends on the generosity of the heart. Of MY *OWN* heart. Through this I also came to understand the process that we call "forgiveness." Nobody else can do it for you.

A separation through death or divorce is not necessarily a punishment or failure. There are no coincidences, only the cause and effect of a universal plan. What I considered to be a failure was only Spirit's way to give me a push ahead telling me to move on, even if I didn't see it that way at the time. A temporary suffering is part of the graduation program that has been created for us, so we will be strong enough to reach the next level. If we can't survive that grief, and instead end up filled with sorrow and bitterness, we may have to go through the process again. And again . . . . and yet again, until we have learned our lesson.

I have found Spirit to be extraordinarily generous in constantly offering us new learning opportunities, until we're finally willing to let go! This is why the world is filled with so much repetition. You see, the same darn thing will happen again and again, until we learn to treat our problem a different way!

During the depth of my deep crisis, when I felt awfully alone and didn't know where to go, I got a helping hand from the most unexpected source, an incident that lasted for only a few seconds, but the effects of those few seconds will never go away. It was one of the biggest moments of my life.

It was an evening like any other evening, and I was walking through my beautiful Florida home, touching the things I'd loved so much and had taken care of during my long marriage. My three Doberman Pinchers were with me, always faithful and full of unlimited joy. The Pomeranian lap dogs were sleeping on the sofa in my bedroom. I was alone at home with many memories of happier times, feeling very uncertain about my future.

Unexpectedly, as I was turning on the lights for the evening, there He was . . . A being coming out of a ray of light, again with that sizzling sound of energy, I could now remember from earlier times in my life, when I had met with the Light. He was dressed the way people were dressed in the Mideast a couple of thousand years ago. I can so well remember the woven texture of His clothing, the end seam by the wrists and the coloring. And I particularly recall how He remained in the light.

Everything happened so fast and I was breathless with surprise. But He stretched his arm towards me, and as He did, I was overwhelmed by an extraordinary warmth. I believe my heart stopped beating as something I can only describe as absolutely selfless Love intensified between us. Without words, He let me know that He was my friend, and that I was part of a plan. He also told me that I was to live that plan, and that everything was going to be alright. I was overwhelmed by the power of His unspoken words and how they had taken an almost magic hold on me.

He disappeared as quickly as He'd appeared. But the Energy of His light remained in the same place for a while, and a glow of energy remained in the air where He'd appeared. As in a trance, I found I couldn't move.

I shall never forget the moment when He appeared before me: I felt as if I'd been lifted out of my body, out of my dimension into a oneness of an indescribable measure. And then I felt such strong . . . Joy! A joy far beyond time. Today, I still feel that joy when I think back to that special moment.

After He left, my arm remained stretched out where He'd appeared, as if our hands had touched each other. I have no idea how long I remained in that position, but I was unable to move and slowly I realized that an unbelievable wave of energy continued to go right through me.

"My God, I met Jesus," I exclaimed out loud. I was so exhilarated, and filled with an energy so indescribably joyous, I thought I could fly, and my feet were literally not touching the floor any more. There was no doubt who He was. He had told me so, and I had "heard" it as if he had said so in the loudest voice.

I was in no way religious. Jesus had never played a role in my life. In fact, none at all. To meet His energy couldn't have been more unexpected.

The happiness of having been touched by this incredible Energy stayed with me for many days and filled me with a sense of completion. What the completion was—I still didn't know in words. Because no words would be large enough to describe our meeting or the feelings that had gone through me during our brief encounter. This was an experience that forever would make a mark on my life. He hadn't told me how to continue my life, only that I was meant to move on and fulfill my plan. No hints about where to go and how to start. But I already knew that the secret to my plan was to keep on going, because as long as I did, everything would soon fall into its right place.

Many feel I should write more about my meeting with the Jesus-Energy, but I can't. Our meeting was an experience so intense and on such a high level, words will only set a limit to my experience.

If I'd been given wings to fly out in the beautiful blue sky and wholeheartedly had enjoyed being lifted up in the air by the wind, how could I then find the words so everyone would understand the wonderful feeling of freedom and connection to the unknown that I had experienced?

After my meeting with the Jesus-Energy, to my surprise an abundance of new possibilities began to open up around me. Seemingly from nowhere, countless new wonderful friends came my way, making my life joyous and happy again. But most of all, my eyes had "cleared" and yet one more time, I could see the unseen. Practically instantly, my gift of seeing and healing had returned to me.

This time, I was grateful for my gift. Finally, I understood the meaning of my gift and where it came from. And I had learned that gifts are meant to be acknowledged, because the one who gave you the gift chose it based on what would be right for you, and this thought is meant to be honored.

This was my Third Awakening.

The presence of the Jesus-Energy has never since then really gone away from my life. Instead, this energy seems to remain close by as a presence of encouragement and protection. To my surprise, soon after the occurrence, I found myself signing up for Divinity school and with time, I became an ordained minister. Considering the life I had led, my decision to do so would seem surprising and even humorous to those who had known me as a busy socialite. But to be a minister was not enough. So, I continued my divinity studies and almost fanatically, as if I had to catch up for lost time, I pulled back almost completely from my previous social life. Three years later, I got my Divinity Doctorate degree, and I was proud. By that time, I knew that things did not just happen coincidentally. *There was definitely a plan for me. As there is a plan for each one of us.* I was now beginning to understand mine.

We can reach our goal when we are "in tune" and we align ourselves with our Higher Intention. Unfortunately, we usually have no idea what this "tune" or Higher Intention is. There is only one way to find out: Move ahead and see for yourself! This may take a few years, but life is all about this continuous movement. When we begin to feel we're in harmony with life and our goals, that's when we're in tune. But, we can only be "in tune" only through our *OWN* experience. Nobody else can do this for us. Nor can any book or success classes. It may sound hard, but it's the only way.

Here is the secret:

To heal, I personally, and nobody else, have to be PART of the transformation process—absolutely unconditionally.

Not only to understand it, but to make it work for me.

This means to let go, and not to judge myself or others of what we can or cannot do. Instead we are to humbly allow that Higher Power to step in and do the work for us.

Yes, I can travel around the world to look for a success formula, but the changes have to occur in MY heart, in MY mind, in MY soul and through MY actions.

I have to let go of the old, learn to forget and learn to make no more judgments. Then I have to forget some more of what may have been hiding deep down in my heart and blocked me from moving forward.

This is what we call forgiveness.

It sometimes also means I have to start from the very beginning.

And this very beginning is:

THE FIRST COMMANDMENT

"You shall have no other Gods before ME."
Follow your I AM. The ME in you.
Spirit in you.
The place that knows all, sees all and hears all . . . .

Be sure of who and what you make Number One in your life, and who and what rules your daily life. Do you know how often you follow the Real Truth or give in to what is more convenient for you at the time?

To understand the first commandment is to feel certain of priorities and to accept the meaning of I AM as the Highest Good, and make this fit into your life.

For you to find your connection to Spirit may take no more than a split second. Because only a very thin veil made up by some deep rooted fixations created by you or your surrounding separates your spiritual self from your physical self.

6

Conversations
with Spirit

The appearance of the Jesus-Energy soon proved
to be a powerful influence on my life. I noticed
that the energy created during that short moment of
spiritual connection, had become part of my very own
spiritual energy, and I began to feel not only more
powerful, but I'd been cleansed in my outlook toward
the world. Because not only had my God-given gift
within me been awakened, I'd also begun to look at
the world with more unconditional openness and less
human emotions or judgment.

But contrary to what many may think, meeting the Jesus-Energy only confirmed my belief that there is only one universal power and that we are all part of this universal oneness. This power is an energy of incredible tolerance that doesn't care who or where we are. And the more we tune in to this power, the more we can become part of *IT*, and *IT* will become part of what we are. This power is the Light within each one of us, and it never goes away, even if we may believe so at times. Nobody, and no religion, can make a special claim on this power. It belongs to everyone.

A few weeks after my meeting with the Jesus-Energy I ended up in the Arizona mountains. I had not planned to go there. In fact, I was supposed to attend a conference in Europe, but somehow Spirit wanted me to be in Arizona at that particular time. I have never believed that so-called coincidence just happened by chance. As I've lived longer and seen more, I've come to the conclusion that what we have looked at as bad or good luck are in fact special plans for us, and that those plans are presented to us through a variety of disguises we sometimes see as luck or even accidents. Most of the time we like to call them coincidences. So, shortly after my arrival in North Arizona, when I was introduced to Rising Sun, a tall and handsome Native American of the venerable Arizona Hopi tribe, I immediately knew that meeting him could only be part of a special plan. And when he mentioned that he'd been given a spiritual message to take me to the sacred grounds of his people, I didn't hesitate to go along.

We met early the following morning. The desert air was still cool, but as the hours went by and we began to climb into the mountains, the hot desert sun began to get the best of me.

"You see those three mountain peaks?" said Rising Sun in his deep voice as he pointed at the impressive rock formations far above us. I nodded, already weakened from the dry heat of the Arizona desert sun.

"We are going all the way up to the top," he added.

"Never, in my life am I going to climb that mountain," I burst out, shaking my head. There was no way I could climb that high.

But he didn't answer me and paid no attention to my hesitation. I had to continue if I liked it or not. I didn't like heights, and the sun was getting so strong that the rock burned my hands. But there was no return. I didn't know my way back and Rising Sun was determined to fulfill his mission to bring me to his holy grounds.

I never thought it would be possible, but finally we did reach the mountain top, and I was amazed to discover the opening to a cave that continued deep into the rock. At one point, I wondered where the light was coming from because the cave wasn't as dark as I'd expected it to be. Right in the center of the cave, Rising Sun sat down beside a well emerging out of the rock. In front of the well, grew a little tree filled with large green leaves.

"This is the tree of life," explained Rising Sun. "This tree and this water have been here since the beginning of time. You are to be initiated by this water and you are to connect with the forces of this tree."

I knelt down by the well as Rising Sun scooped water into his hand. With words I can no longer remember, he poured the water over my head.

What happened next I can hardly remember. As in a dream I found myself separated from my body floating among purple pyramids, with the feeling that I was beyond all time. I believed I heard sounds of what could've been music, but I wasn't sure. All I cared about was that I wanted to stay in that place.

I had no idea how much time had passed when Rising Sun touched my shoulder and told me it was time to leave. As we left the cave, the day had gone by and the sun was already descending behind the mountain tops. I felt so light and youthful and had no idea what had happened, but somehow it appeared I'd been awakened from a long, long sleep.

Coming back to Florida, I was confused. Why did so many strangers suddenly contact me for healing and advice? Where did they come from? How did they know where to find me? Although I loved helping each one of them, I wasn't sure I wanted any part of this activity. They expected so much from me, and I wasn't sure I was willing to handle the responsibility. I was particularly concerned that social society, where I had been a leader for so long, would find my unusual activities unacceptable. One more time in my life, I tried to push away what I was really all about. And yet again, I made the conditions of my exterior life override the passion of my *TRUE* self. Was I ever going to learn?

Deeply bewildered, and not understanding where I belonged any more, every evening before sunset, I would walk on the sandy South Florida beaches asking myself what I was all about. What was my purpose? Was this really the life I was born to live? Somewhere within me I felt conflict, but I didn't know exactly why and where. And as I allowed the incoming ocean waves to wash over my bare feet, I debated with my Higher Self about how I could heal the conflict that was building up within me. And I lifted my eyes to the heavens and asked "Why? Why Me?"

"Why have you put me in this situation?" I asked. "I used to be free to do with my life as I pleased. I like having the insight and the knowledge, but I don't think I'm ready to help all the sick and needy of the world. Please not this way. And not now. Maybe not ever. I am not ready to accept this responsibility."

And again I felt like a child who had trouble leaving the security of family and home, unwilling to start life on her own.

But I received no reply from the Heavens. I tried to look for clues in the big Florida sky that toward the evening usually was filled with several layers of light clouds, but there was still no sign of help.

Many weeks went by. The weeks turned into months.

"Why is this happening to me? Why do I have to go through this ordeal?" I asked again, and again and lifted my eyes to the big sky as if it would open up and send me a big sign for the right solution. "Why?" I repeated. "Tell me why!"

"Because of the one you are!" I suddenly heard.

What was *THAT*? Amazed to finally receive an answer, I sat down in the sand and watched the sky above me. I needed to think. Had I heard right? And what did that answer mean?

"Could you please be more specific?" I asked.

"Because of what you have chosen to do since the beginning of your time."

I wasn't sure how to take this. I had hoped for directions that I would have no trouble understanding.

"But this is not what I want to do," I objected.

"Oh yes, it is."

"Of course not. What are people going to say when I do things they don't understand and can find no proof for?"

"It is their problem, not yours."

"But . . . I DON'T WANT TO DO IT!!"

"Well, then you die!"

"What????"
"If you don't do this, you'll die!"

"I thought you were loving and kind God."

"I am."

"But you said, you'll kill me if I don't do this work?"

"No, I didn't. I said you would die."

"Isn't that the same?"

"No, I have never killed anyone. People kill in my name. But I never do."

"So, what do you mean?"

"You'll die because if you don't pursue your heart's, or your soul's desire, you'll lose your purpose for being on this Earth. You don't know this, but in your soul you are already programmed to do the work. You have now only just begun. If you don't follow your soul's desire, you will soon lose the purpose for living, and you will attract a reason for leaving this world you have learned to call yours."

"I'm confused. Let me think for a while."

"I gave you the free will to choose, you know. But you have been made to believe by your society that your human thought is a Master in making the right choices. This isn't always so. Your true choice is already in your heart . . . and has been since the beginning of your time."

"But I don't want to do this kind of work!"

"Yes, in your soul, you do, and you know it. This is the conflict you are now going through."

"But I can't. What are people going to say? They

have respected me for all the good I have done for the community. Now they will think I've gone insane."

"Then THEY need help!"

"But how do you know I am worthy of doing what you ask me to do?"

"Why do you think I have given you all these visions, and all those lessons and constant reminders, time after time? And those special moments when I saved your life, so you could stay in your world just a little while longer . . . . You mean you haven't noticed?"

We continued our conversations for weeks, maybe even for months, and I was getting more and more impatient. Time was standing still around me. But then, all of a sudden, everything that had happened in my life made perfect sense: Childhood, motherhood, widowhood and all those endless, sometimes far-out choices, constantly offering themselves to me, so I would not only discover more, but also understand more, learn more. And I understood why my life had been saved from disaster so many times.

"OK, OK," I said. "I'll do it. I'll use my gift the way it was intended to be used from the beginning." Then I paused a little and added: *"I promise. Yes, I DO promise!"* And this time I meant it. I felt in my heart, this was my true wish. There was no going back.

As soon as I made that commitment, a weight was taken off my chest and I felt so young and light, and deliriously happy. Full of deep relief, I danced across the sandy beach.

"Finally, I'm free and I can be the one I was meant to be!" I wanted to call out loud so the whole world could hear. And I realized that, with my deep-set attitudes, I had caused all the doubt and confusion in my life. What a beautiful life I was going to have! How I looked forward to fulfilling the mission I was meant to do. When I looked up at the sky again, I was surprised to see that the sky had already turned dark, and how the full moon covered the ocean with a remarkable silver light. It was late and I'd opened a new door in my life. It was now time to go home.

I had made my commitment and I was relieved. There were no more questions to ask. I had made my pledge, and I was prepared to walk my path. Nobody knew about my conversations with Spirit during those few months, nor about my reluctance to get involved, and about my final commitment. But from that evening on, my heart was filled with peace, and I was grateful for the gift and the mission I'd been given.

I loved my work and my life. I was soon to be known as the Doctor of Divinity of all faiths, who'd been blessed with a divine seeing and healing gift. And the more I worked, the stronger and better I felt, although I sometimes had calls from those in need around the clock. I had no idea how they found me, but I loved being there for them. Because I now understood one thing:

True healing can only be performed one way, and that is the way of unconditional love.

Or to be more specific:

True healing is a process of Love, where unconditional energy is sent from my unconditional heart, and is received by YOUR equally unconditional heart.

True healing is a letting go of any kind of judgment. Not only in my giving, but particularly in your receiving. Because when you let go and are able to receive, this is the time when Spirit, the Light, in you will eagerly open all possible doors for your inner Self to activate.

This is the way and the truth about what is taking place.

7

Breaking Away from the Past

As soon as I'd made the commitment to Spirit to finally pursue the work that was intended for me, I enjoyed practically instant success. People came from faraway places for alternative help after nothing else they had tried seemed to help. They came not only for physical challenges, but often they also had serious problems with themselves or unfinished issues with others. I genuinely loved my work and I was convinced that I'd found both my life's mission and purpose. It was also obvious why my life had been saved so many times.

"What is your method?" asked many who had heard of my work, and were now curious.

"There is no method," I would answer. "As people sit comfortably and fully dressed in front of me, I connect with Spirit, and without touching them, their very own personal blueprint intuitively pops up in front of me on an imaginary screen. In this blueprint I see an outline of their physical and emotional problems as well as their predispositions. I also find visions of old memories, sometimes dating back to other lifetimes, that today are still painful for the soul and may be the cause for both sickness and unhappiness in this lifetime. Then, through the power of Spirit, their own healing ability, that core of Light within each one of us, is awakened and as long as they allow it to happen a process of healing is set into motion. It's that simple."

"What do you mean by past life memories?"

"Memories are energy. We are energy-beings and are influenced by all energies, both good ones and not so good ones, and these energies don't always go away, once we've attracted them. Thoughts and emotions are energy. Some emotions are more painful than others and will eventually become part of us, since energy never dies. They may even remain through many lifetimes. I have found that many physical ailments, *particularly* the very serious ones, have been triggered by painful memories deep down in the soul."

I've also noticed that some physical conditions have been caused by some kind of trauma in this lifetime, and that this has created an imbalance of energy-waves in the brain, sending unusual symptoms to other parts of the body. Intuitively, I see those brain-energies as curls that need to be straightened out or tied together. Once this has been done—as amazing as it may sound—the physical condition has been greatly improved, in some cases even completely healed. "

Not for a minute do I take credit for the knowledge that comes through me. I am just an instrument for Spirit, with a mission to awaken the healing power within each one of us. At times, a positive change occurs almost immediately, but often the healing process is gradual, and can depend on your willingness to participate in the healing. After all, true healing is done by *"your OWN inner self."*

Although my work was successful and I received much gratitude from so many, I was often overcome by deep fear during my working hours, as if I was doing something very wrong and forbidden. Sometimes my fear was so strong I could hardly breathe. And all the time I envisioned how the police would violently break down my door, beat me up, tie my arms and take me away. Why I felt this way, I could not explain.

As the months went by, my feelings of wrongdoing and fear increased. I was confused. Evidently, my new profession had triggered a very sensitive part of my soul. Because soon I perceived in greater detail how a group of armed men, wearing dark uniforms of medieval times and representing the government, had broken down my door and arrested me. I had screamed and didn't understand. After they had tied my hands, I was taken away, and then the scene blacked out. I could see no further. Those historical flashbacks didn't make sense to me, but they began to disrupt my work. At no time did it occur to me that those images could be residues of a past life memory, and that now they'd begun to create a new, and very intruding, "parallel reality" for me, along with the life I already lived. Nor did it occur to me that it was important to have this unwanted "reality" removed, and that I might have to heal myself for a change!

I discussed this situation with Charlie Anderson, a Lutheran minister, and a good friend, as we spent a few hours together on a Sunday afternoon for lunch and good conversation. When he was about to leave, he made a remark that I shall never forget, because his words made me open my eyes. In an instant, I understood that you cannot be a good healer until you have healed yourself!

"A tragic memory of a past life is blocking you," Charlie commented spontaneously as he was on his way out. "You have to get rid of this memory, before it gets rid of you," he continued, but explained nothing else. A bit bewildered and without asking any questions, I gave him my usual hug goodbye, and he drove off, waving cheerfully.

I was surprised by what he said. I hadn't expected this from Charlie. Past lives did not belong to the principles of his Church. But on the other hand, he sometimes dared leave the opinions of his Church behind for what he felt was the ultimate truth. Because he knew that we are energy-beings, that energy never dies, and that everything we experience, may it be good or not so good, goes into a bank of memories, located "somewhere within our being." Those memories accumulate in our bank of cellular memories and build up a strong pile of banking interests that later may take a strong hold on us and begin to interfere with our lives.

With Charlie's words still ringing in my ears, I couldn't help thinking back to my daily routine and had to admit that a wall of fear had been building up around me each time, I was in a session with a client, and I began to find it hard to take. Just as Charlie had said, somewhere within me there was blockage, and it had to be removed soon, or it would indeed stop me from being a good intuitive healer and messenger. If I couldn't use fully my connection to Spirit, I wouldn't be able to accomplish the mission I'd been given in this lifetime.

What I usually would do only for others, I now practiced on myself: I sat down in my study, and with the same method I would use in my daily work, I relaxed my body and mind and put myself entirely and unconditionally in the hands of my Higher Self. I surrounded myself totally in the White Light, and then unconditionally, with no expectations, I slowly allowed myself to sink back into my own memory bank. The intensity and reality of my experience was amazing, as I let go and allowed myself to be carried away into the secrets of my past.

I saw myself in Spain in the middle ages, during the time of the Spanish Inquisition. A time when thousands of innocent citizens, mostly women, were arrested in the name of the Church, because they were considered a threat to the Church one way or the other. Under the

pressure of severe torture, they were made to confess to their sins, and then, with big pomp and fanfare, they were executed in public. But as the wife of a prominent nobleman, who was an avid financial supporter of the Catholic Church, I believed I was safe. We lived in Madrid in a large palace-like home surrounded by a high iron fence. A uniformed guard stood at the entrance opening and closing the gates when necessary. I could see it so clearly. And I sensed how I was deeply religious and how I visited the Cathedral every day, to light a candle and to say my prayers.

As I looked at the tall rod iron fence again, I discovered a line of people standing outside the gate. And I perceived how they had come to see me from far way places hoping to be helped by my intuitive healing powers. By looking at these images, I "knew" all about my life, as if I lived it all over again. And I also knew that my husband would often travel, but that I would stay at home, continuing my work to help the sick and needy.

As the years passed, certain members of the clergy and the so-called medical profession of the time were becoming disgruntled. Hardly anybody came to see them any more, and instead a steady stream of patients were coming through my opened gate. But the Church and the learned dared say nothing since my husband was a powerful and very wealthy man, and always very generously had supported the ruling institutions of Spain.

But then my husband died, and my life took a dramatic turn. One day as I was working as usual, dark-clad soldiers forced themselves through the big gate, broke down the big wooden front door, and forcefully pulled me away from my beautiful home. I was interrogated about my healing activities in front of the Tribunal and the judges tried to force me to say that my abilities were given to me by the devil. But I refused. I trusted Spirit, and knew that the help that others had received through me could only come from the Highest Good of the Heavens.

Then I was tortured terribly, but my tormentors finally gave up, and called for the Grand Inquisitor to personally continue the abuse of my physical body. I still refused to admit any guilt, and was not willing to sell my soul for mercy.

"Bruja, you witch," screamed the Grand Inquisitor almost exploding of fury. "You are impossible. I don't get

anywhere with you," he said as he continued to torment me.

What was left of me after the series of ghastly tortures was barely alive. But the Grand Inquisitor decided my life was to end in a blazing fire in front of the Cathedral not far from my home, which after my arrest had been confiscated and now belonged to the Church. The public was meant to watch me burn to understand what would happen when you went against the power of the Church.

Slowly, the flames consumed all that used to be me, and my name was meant to be forgotten . . . .

I opened my eyes. What had happened to me? I was still in my study with soft music playing in the background. But I was soaking wet from perspiration and emotions. And I was trembling and crying profoundly.

It was already dark outside and I wondered where all the time had gone. I'd never gone through anything quite like this before. But what had happened to me living a life as noblewoman during the Spanish Inquisition felt so real, and the experience suddenly explained so many of my feelings and fears I hadn't understood before: When I first visited Spain, I panicked and almost fainted when a group of uniformed soldiers walked past me in the street. But most of all, it explained why I was so fearful of being arrested when I was working. I didn't want to go through that pain again. How clearly I could see it now.

I cried uncontrollably as the past suffering poured out of me. All the injustice and pain was finally surfacing into the open, ready to be washed away by the Light. I continued to cry as, before my inner eyes, I watched the slender, dark-haired woman who had been such a strong influence on my own energy. And I allowed her feelings to become part of my feelings, as we together went through the process of healing in the soul we somehow shared. In awe I saw what happened to me after I died in that past life. It seemed so unbelievably real:

I was suddenly swept into the energy of the White Light and I enjoyed the brightness and warmth of the Light. How I had longed for this to happen! Peace now flowed through me again, and I felt released from all the pain and darkness of the past. But I had one final wish that I needed to fulfill before I was ready to find eternal peace: I wanted my soul to be blessed by my beloved Church. By order by the Tribunal from the Grand Inquisitor, I had been denied any kind of spiritual blessing at the time of my physical passing. I was still grieving this, still believing I had been rejected by the Heavens. But Spirit heard my wish . . . and with the power of the Light, my grief was forever taken away. Quietly and very softly, I was lifted into the Light and placed in the dimensions beyond what we call time.

Spirit had now brought me back into my beloved Cathedral, where I was placed in an open coffin in front of the altar, which was covered with white flowers. An iridescent white Light began to shine around me, and somehow I knew that the Light was meant to cleanse, and to help me forgive and forget. I was so relieved to be inside the Cathedral. With the glow of white Light shining all over me, I just couldn't stop crying. And I cried and cried.

I remained in the Light for a long time, as if I needed to be convinced that I was safe. And in my soul I wished to make sure that I was forgiven . . . in the soul we both had in common. That was why I cried so much.

All of a sudden the Light around me grew more intense and I felt so light and bright. Then, quietly, a beam of intense Light lifted me from my open coffin and I was raised through the air into the Big White Light.

"I had come home."

Finally, I was freed from my past. I was healed. And I had found my peace.

In healing my past, I had also healed my present. I now understood the cause for my fear, and that the unexplainable anxiety I'd experienced earlier during my healing sessions was an energy remnant of my past. Facing it again and being able to remove it felt like I had spring-cleaned a dirty closet filled with old debris. Incredibly relieved, I immediately fell asleep on the sofa in my den with all the lights on, and soft music still playing. I had just re-arranged and completed the end of another life.

We are energy, and as energy-beings we attract energy.
Everything that happens to us in our lives is energy.
No matter when, where and how we live.
Energy never dies.
Therefore, our past is still part of what we are today, and can possibly influence our lives much more than we realize.

For no reason at all, the next morning I called my local telephone company and asked for my telephone number to be exchanged for a new one. Later in the day I found myself changing all the codes on my alarm systems as well as all bank access numbers. I had no idea why.

I did not discover until much later that since birth, we have been assigned a particular "energy-code" to live by. This "code" is defined in our blueprint, and will determine the ease with which we will live our lives and how we pursue our goals. But since I had now been healed and removed a blockage of pain and fear in my past, I had become part of a new and better plan and therefore was assigned a new energy-code with a much higher possibility for success. Because, again, we're a product of a careful plan of "cause and effect," in which everything in our past and presence is coordinated. For things to happen a certain way, you must maintain a certain high-level harmony balance that we, at this point, are unable to comprehend logically.

But the story doesn't end there. It gets even more incredible because Spirit's imagination is absolutely phenomenal. Each time we're taken one step further than before—just to show us that there is no such thing as "knowing it all!"

At that time I was engaged to be married to Henry, a very conservative British barrister and Q.C., a Queen's Counsel. He worked internationally, but maintained a head office in London. We had had a brief relationship before I met Jack. After my divorce from Jack, Henry and I activated our friendship as if we had some unfinished business between us, and we got engaged to be married.

Henry didn't believe in my work. He lived his everyday life as if he was trying to prove a case in court and only believed in issues that could be backed up with written proof and that he had accepted as valuable knowledge. Whereas I was free to think and act outside the limitations of conventional opinion, he had great trouble doing so. He often told me that he disapproved of my work, and was glad that at that time I practiced in other countries and not officially in England.

After I'd removed the blockages of wrong-doing and fear from my soul, I felt so incredibly well that I wanted to share my experience with Henry in one of our daily telephone calls across the Atlantic. But each time I mentioned the phrase "past life," he cut me off and changed the subject without giving me a chance to explain what the past life experience was all about. So, naturally, I was flabbergasted when Henry called me from his London penthouse apartment a few days later. It was after midnight in Miami and I was ready to go to bed. He had just awakened to a new day. I was soon to find out—in more ways than one.

Henry was crying. I'd never heard him like this before.

"I just woke up from a terrible dream," he sobbed. "You probably won't believe it, but I was the Grand Inquisitor during the Spanish Inquisition. I had you arrested and I tortured you terribly. It was just awful what I did to you."

I couldn't believe my ears, and I knew I must have listened to him with my mouth open. Henry was telling me what *I* had experienced in *MY VERY OWN* regression! How could this be possible? He had refused to listen to my story, and had never given me a chance to tell him one word about it. And now he was telling me *MY* story! That *SAME* story I had just "lived" through! Without me telling him a word about it, he already knew everything.

"I did dreadful things to you, I called you terrible things and kept on hurting you. And when you wouldn't cooperate, and admit to your sins, I gave the order for you to be burned in front of everyone," Henry continued.

"But this is the story *I* wanted to tell *YOU*," I interrupted, but he didn't seem to hear me.

"Can you please, forgive me . . . ," he continued, still crying. "I need your help. There is so much I don't understand. And everything was so real, I felt it and saw it. I know it was true. Please, please I am so sorry . . . ."

I was in shock. Henry, the mastermind of intellect, was in tears and asking me for forgiveness for what he did to me in a . . . dream! But of course, I knew his dream couldn't have been a dream. Because his dream had, in its entirety, coincided with my regression. I was speechless. Of course there is no such thing as coincidence, only a falling into place of events.

But, in an instant, everything made perfect sense. I had found our connection, and why we had been so inexplicably drawn to each other when we met the very first time. Although I had believed I loved and respected Henry for his many talents, I now understood why I could never quite relax in his company.

Somehow, I always had to prove my case when I was with him. Also, Henry loved Spain, spoke fluent Spanish, and owned a villa in the South of Spain. I, on the other hand, usually felt slightly sick when I visited Spain and had trouble speaking the language although I was a linguist. I speak and write several languages, and can usually make conversation in a few more when needed.

And I recalled many times, when during our tender moments, Henry had looked me in the eyes and said, "Bruja."

"What does Bruja mean," I asked in the beginning, and he would look surprised as if I had taken him out of a trance.

"Oh, did I say Bruja? Oh, it means witch in Spanish, but I wouldn't call you that. I love you," he'd answered. And we both wondered why he unconsciously and so often would call me witch in Spanish, a language that had nothing to do with our present relationship.

I now knew.

Yes, all the pieces now began to fall into place. Spirit yet one more time had shown us that we're all are part of an incredible Oneness, in which everything is possible and all and everything is connected. What we've learned to call "time" is part of a Oneness, in which there are absolutely no boundaries. Time actually doesn't matter, because it doesn't exist in the higher dimensions. And a chip of that Oneness exists within all of us.

Several days went by without Henry's regular daily call. I had a feeling he was embarrassed after having shown me such deep emotions, so I left him alone to digest his feelings. When he finally called me up, he was distant, and his voice was almost cold and businesslike. Gone were the tears, the confession and the plea for forgiveness.

"I don't want you to continue your work after we are married," he announced almost immediately. He tried to convince me that it was wrong for someone of my background to practice a profession he regarded as unacceptable, mainly because the work couldn't be substantiated by scientific proof.

"There is no proof for an experience. It is beyond the limitation of written proof," I insisted and shook my head. And I asked what had happened to his dream, his tearful regrets and his wishes to learn more, only three days earlier?

"Nonsense, absolute nonsense." He raised his voice and was irritated that I'd brought it up.

"But your dream and my experience with my past life were both the same," I protested. "You know very well they were not a coincidence. I never brought up any of the circumstances regarding my past life. You did. I didn't see you as the Grand Inquisitor. You did. I didn't bring up the Spanish Inquisition with the pain and torture. You did. Don't you realize you and I have now been brought together so we can heal and forgive our past?" I continued, surprised at his complete change of heart.

But Henry ignored my remarks:

"Rubbish, forget it. I am not going to change anything I was brought up to believe in," he continued in the same agitated tone ". . . and you shouldn't deal with matters you cannot prove!"

Suddenly, I felt as if we were way back in the past, where I had to defend my beliefs one more time. And I saw Henry as the Grand Inquisitor who was stuck in one small room, with no windows to look through and no door to walk out from, making it impossible for him to understand what's going on outside. *He* was the prisoner, unable to leave his locked up room. *I* was free. I was allowed to use my own eyes and my own mind to explore and expand. Was I ever the lucky one!

I knew that Spirit sometimes shows us the truth in what we believe are dreams, since dreams are more acceptable to us. It's easier that way.

I now clearly recognized my purpose with Henry. Yes, I had forgiven him with all my heart, but the time had now come for me to move on. And this time I was free to go. Henry couldn't stop me now. And the feeling to be free to go suddenly made me feel so incredibly rich and joyous.

"You're trying to control me again, just like you did once before," I told Henry, already enjoying the taste of a new future without him, a life where I wouldn't be limited regarding what I said, thought, or believed in. "You know, we had different philosophies then, and as you notice, we still do today. You've stopped me from my work before and you're trying to do it again. It seems nothing much has changed," I continued. "But you couldn't stop me from my beliefs then. And you can't do it now. I have to follow the Light that shines in my soul."

"No, you are wrong, absolutely, abominably wrong . . . and you don't understand," Henry almost screamed through the telephone. I couldn't comprehend why he was so angry, and I felt our exchange of philosophical differences was not getting anywhere.

I had known for a long time that there is no particular "one" right or wrong faith that everyone in the world is willing to understand. Belief is a process of never-ending awakenings. How we believe depends on our own state of mind, and our own connection with Spirit. Nobody has the right to force their beliefs on others. And I was sure of one thing: The way I had permitted Spirit to take over in my life had brought me so much further than the pages in a book could possibly do. And I told him so.

"You, Bruja, you are impossible. I don't get anywhere with you," Henry angrily screamed through the telephone. His voice went through me like the cut of a knife directly in my heart. I knew he was unaware that he'd called me *Bruja* again.

I suddenly felt nauseous. Those had been the exact words I had heard from of the Grand Inquisitor, when only a few days earlier I had regressed back to my past life during the Spanish Inquisition.

Yes, I was now certain that our relationship had been arranged by Spirit, "the Power that sees all and knows all," and that our relationship had been necessary for my highest good, so I could strengthen my Trust in a Higher Power. For me, our purpose for being together was now completed. Whether *his* purpose was completed or not wasn't up to me to determine. It was up to Spirit to decide. Our relationship had never been a mistake. It was meant to be, but not to continue any further.

So I felt no regrets when I said goodbye to Henry. I could only wish him well and send him off into the loving hands of the Universe, where sometime and somewhere, he would again meet the challenge of learning unconditional love. He and I were not meant to be husband and wife. At least not in this lifetime.

What is unconditional love? We could explain it for pages and pages, but the answer is very simple. You have to live it to understand it. Because unconditional love is simply this:

To let go of human judgment and to use
an open mind.
To understand that we are all part of
an incredible Oneness.
This Oneness includes absolutely everyone and
absolutely everything.
And what is "right" and what is "wrong" is
up to Spirit to decide.

8

They Witnessed the Light

What is that White Light that time after time has so surprisingly intervened in my life? The truth is simple: the White Light is the Activation of Spirit in each one of us. The White Light is a vibrational frequency of an energy so high we can only comprehend it as a presence of . . . *LIGHT*. This energy is the essence of what we truly are, and I connect with it in prayer before each working session for both inspiration and protection. Our divine purpose here on Earth is to enhance our natural connection to this power and to use it as our capital of unlimited resources.

For me it took almost a whole lifetime to find that out.

One amazing event showed Spirit's enormous power and ingenuity: This time Spirit appeared in front of witnesses as . . . *a bolt of light.*

During the years when I was married to Jack, my life consisted of lots of Florida sunshine and a whirl of travel, beautiful social get-togethers and charity functions. Since I enjoyed charity work and was regarded as a good organizer, I was often asked to be the Chairperson for a variety of glamorous charity events.

This particular event celebrated the season opening for our regional South Florida Philharmonic Orchestra at a venerable Florida hotel. Everyone was invited, the Maestro of international fame, community leaders, sponsors of the orchestra and of course anyone willing to pay the price for a charity event. And I was the Chairperson, in charge of everything, including my very own welcoming speech.

Only minutes before the doors to the beautifully decorated party room were going to open to the several hundred guests who were having cocktails on the patio outside, I was inside the room, standing in front of a table making last minute notes on my many checklists. Some committee members had already arrived and were socializing on the other side of the room across from me, waiting for the doors to open so they could greet the incoming guests.

Somewhere in the back of my mind, I believed I heard someone scream on the other side of the room, but I was too absorbed with my paperwork to even raise my head to find out the reason for the scream.

Only a split second later, I heard an incredible crash. Irritated, I turned around toward the noise. I didn't want anything to go wrong before the opening of my event, and the noise definitely sounded like trouble.

Just as I turned around, a small, but very sharp, piece of something that I couldn't see too well, flew through the air and made a deep cut on my right hand. It was a piece of mirrored glass, and I was amazed to discover that a large section of the mirrored wall in front of me had completely detached itself from the wall. But instead of falling straight down to crush me and cut me apart under its sharp weight, it had made a 90-degree plunge far away from me—as if it had bounced off me. When it fell to the floor, it broke into a thousand pieces.

"Oh my God, this is a miracle, this is a miracle," screamed a beautiful tall woman as she came rushing up to me. It was Gloria, one of my committee members. Behind her came Julia, the social writer for one of our local newspapers.

"Are you all right?" Gloria gasped, looking at my hand, which was now bleeding.

I didn't understand. Why was she so excited about a small cut on my hand? I wondered why everyone looked so bewildered.

"We couldn't understand why it happened, but we saw how the one of the mirrored sections of the wall suddenly unglued itself from the wall and was about to fall down over you. We were across from you on the other side of the room and we tried to warn you, but you didn't hear us," Gloria continued. She was still trembling and couldn't stop talking.

"And when the mirror was just about to hit you . . . Oh my God, you would have been killed . . . Suddenly there was this bolt of White Light . . . jumping out of you . . . between you and the mirror . . . Can you believe it? . . . A bolt of Light? . . . As if it was a hand of Light . . . It threw the mirror away from you, and you were saved!"

Gloria was so shaken she had to catch her breath. It was hard for her to believe that she had witnessed something she would call a miracle.

Overwhelmed, I looked at the rumble of crushed mirror covering the floor, maybe thirty-five feet away from me, where stunned waiters were already sweeping away all the broken pieces. Nobody could understand it. How did the mirror get there? And as I looked at my bleeding hand, I not only knew that the pieces of the mirrored glass were as sharp as razor blades, I also realized that Spirit wanted to remind me of our connection. Yes, indeed this was a miracle. Without hesitation, I knew I'd been protected from a terrible accident.

Gloria, the well-known socialite, now an instant believer in the spiritual, wanted everyone to know what had happened, and kept on repeating our experience with the mirror to new onlookers. But they all remained silent, and in disbelief they soon walked away. On the other hand, Julia, the journalist, heavy-set and known for her jovial calm, had quietly gone to sit down at a nearby table. Mystified, she had not uttered one word.

"Now, you'll have a good story to write about," I smiled at Julia a few minutes later as I passed by her on my way to greet the many arriving guests.

"I can't," Julia answered and shook her head. "I think I'll be fired if I do. You see, this isn't the kind of story my editor would ever want to publish. Nobody is going to believe a word I say, and they'll only think I made it up."

Sadly, I knew she was right. Even those who had witnessed the incident with their own eyes preferred not to talk about it to anyone else. Some didn't even know if they could trust what they'd seen.

I had no time for comments. Instead, it was important for me to return to my duties as Chairperson for such an elegant affair, and I was concerned about making "my" social event the success that everyone had expected from me. So, only seconds later, I was back at the door, greeting guests, smiling at photographers who were taking my picture for the social pages, and saying the same unimportant little things, in a world where I knew my name would be soon forgotten.

But Spirit, on the other hand, had clearly made a point of not forgetting me. Throughout my life I hadn't given much care or attention to our relationship, and now years later, I realize the incredible patience and tolerance that Spirit had shown me one time after the other. Never giving up on me and always giving me yet another chance . . . .

Of course, I was deeply grateful for the miracle Spirit had sent me, instantly saving me from the falling mirror, but most of all I was unbelievably impressed that it had happened at all. And, for a few moments, I felt bright waves of warmth—it felt like deep love—go through me, and with the brightness and warmth I was reminded of that night in my bedroom at Lake Wolfgang in the Austrian Alps where the Light had spoken to me for so long.

Perhaps the Light had spoken to me this time too, and maybe it had tried to remind me that I'd left my mission behind when I married Jack. At that time, I had so many people who were all grateful for the help they'd received through me and they'd asked me to return. But I never did. Maybe Spirit had created this special opportunity for me to open my eyes, reminding me of something I had pushed away so often. And then I wondered, why was my healing right hand cut and now bleeding so hard?

What was the bolt of Light that had jumped out of me just in time to save me from the deadly mirror?

Eventually, I understood the basic *Truth*: The Light that had jumped out of me was my *own* Light, the activation of Spirit in *me*. But this time Spirit had carefully chosen to appear in front of others so *they* could remind me of its existence. Because at that time, I trusted their eyes more than mine. What they had seen with *THEIR* eyes was the proof I needed to accept that there is such a thing as the Light, and indeed I now believed we had a very special relationship.

The Light is the "Balance of All That Is." When all energies of "all and everything" accumulate at the highest of frequency, there will be a rotation of . . . White Light. This is what is called the *"Perfection."*

In the "Perfection" there is absolutely everything. How could it be the Perfection if it didn't know all sides, all heights and all depths, all joys and all sorrow, all riches and all poverty? . . . And how would I be part of any perfection if I hadn't seen the valleys of pain, *as well as* enjoying the pleasures of life?

And finally I had to learn that to survive without the hurt we have to leave our feelings of misfortune in the hands of unconditional love. This means: don't judge your life, yourself and others based on your human emotions, intellectual knowledge or social programming.

Unfortunately, we've been made to believe that spiritual knowledge is complicated and is reserved only for those who've been schooled in the subject. But this is far from the truth. Spiritual knowledge already lives within us, and a natural bond exists between each one of us and this knowledge. Everything depends on our own personal relationship with Spirit, and it's never up to others to judge our relationship with Spirit or what *we* make out of it. Meeting with Spirit is always a one-on-one connection, and only you, alone, can experience Spirit your way. We don't have to go through anyone else to be with Spirit. Your own *SINCERE INTENTION* to be together is good enough.

And as we live our *INTENTION* to align with the Spirit Light, we'll develop a bond between us and the Light, and we'll gradually be brought to a level of insights that are higher than what we've ever known before. If, on the other hand, our *INTENTION* is unclear or full of doubt, we might unintentionally turn the wrong switch and nothing will happen at all, except for maybe some more doubt, or whatever else was on your mind.

To connect with the Light is as simple as singing a single tone. It is not necessary to sing the whole song. Because when we try too hard to find our connection to the Light, it means we're not trusting our ability to do so and instead try to bring in our human intellect.

Our intellect is more wanting than it is trusting and it will make us believe we have to connect with the Light many times—almost like turning on a switch back and forth—so it works better.

But it doesn't!

This is merely the way of our logic and not the way Spirit responds to our needs. Spirit is direct and to the point, and Spirit never, never doubts. And Spirit always heard you the first time!

9

Life Is a Constant Awakening

As I did often in the early morning, I was walking along the sandy beaches of Miami Beach. The night had been stormy, and a heavy surf rolled in over the sand as I watched a few brown pelicans make deep dives into the water to catch yet another fish out of the rough waves. The morning was overcast with heavy gray layers of clouds covering the rising sun, and the breeze was quite cool for an April morning in South Florida. The beach was deserted, and I enjoyed the company of the wind, the sand and the ocean. I was in a good mood and felt grateful for the way my life had turned out.

A few years had now passed since I'd been healed from my past lifetime wounds of almost four hundred years ago, when I'd had to endure false accusations and torture during the Spanish Inquisition. After those memories, not only did my life immediately change for the better, but my spiritual abilities also increased in strength and I began to experience an inner satisfaction and feeling of completion I'd never known before. The reason for my being on this earth at this time in history suddenly made sense, and the path I was to follow appeared so obvious and uncomplicated.

"You know, in my subconscious I was scared of having to go through the same pain again, and this stopped me from being the one I was meant to be in this lifetime," I used to tell others when I found that they, too, were plagued by painful past life experiences.

"We are energy beings and since energy never dies, the imprints of those past experiences will remain in some secret dimension of our being. They will never go away until they're changed, one way or the other," I tried to explain.

"You mean we can change memories?" they would then ask.

"Yes, of course, energies can be reconditioned and images of darkness and hurt can be changed into memories of light and happiness. You see, we're part of an energy continuum, where there is no end-station. There is always a continuum to what we are and what we can do." I would answer.

And they would ask what life was all about.

Yes, what was the meaning of my life? And what is the meaning of everyone's life? When and where does it start? When are we supposed to find the true meaning of our lives? From the day we were born? A bit later? When later? Where do we come from? And where are we going?

This is the shocking truth: Our life was given to us in order to find out, and we're constantly led into situations, where it's up to each one of us to learn how to handle our particular situation. The way we look at our lives and deal with our situation—that's what separates the winners from the non-winners. Through our particular choice we'll eventually discover for ourselves, why things happen a certain way, and what it's all about. And if we don't learn the first time, we'll be placed in the same situation again and again, until in the end we make a different choice and finally learn to go a different way. Our purpose as human beings is to *REFINE* our connection to the Light in a process that only Spirit and each individual can experience directly *TOGETHER*. Sometimes this may take a long time because of our free will to satisfy our human "greed and fear," which may often interfere with our original intention.

I sat down for a while on the damp sand. I closed my eyes, and allowed the wind to sweep over my face. The beach was still empty of other people, and I liked it that way. My work was successful, but I felt I'd come to a standstill with my book. What else was I going to write about? My work? About the many interesting case stories from different corners of the world? About discovering that people from the same country appeared to have similar soul memories? That often a deformed body has been given as a *GIFT*, and not a punishment? About the miraculous recovery of a head of state, who naturally will remain nameless, since my work is highly confidential? About the movie star who needed to get rid of his drug habits: He threw up all night after our session and hasn't touched drugs since. About the little girl, who for weeks was fading away and no one in the medical field knew what was wrong with her. Nor did I, but I saw "an energy" that didn't belong in her stomach. Through connecting with Spirit, it was removed, and two days later, she was back in school. Or the young couple looking for help because the wife was unable to conceive? Ten months later, she gave birth to a bouncing baby girl.

There was so much I wanted to share with the world. So many visions and meetings with the Light, sometimes too close to my heart to mention to others. And the many success stories, where through the power of Spirit, "I" had helped and healed. So many now lived happy and healthy lives again . . . There was so much to tell and so much to share.

"How shall I continue?" I heard myself call out loud, as I looked over the ocean and saw the white-capped waves hitting the sand. "What shall I say? There are so many directions I would like to take."

"Maybe you have written enough!"

I was startled. I looked around me and saw that I was alone. I hadn't heard the voice of Spirit for a while.

"But what I wrote is so short," I protested. "People like details. They want long explanations. They believe they learn more from big, lengthy books even if they don't ever read the whole thing."

"That's the problem."

"What do you mean?"

"*Too many words. Words won't take them anywhere. The Truth is very, very simple.*"

"But how will they know what the Truth is?"

"*To know the Truth, you have to LIVE it. Not until then can you say that you know the truth.*"

"But they feel they need instructions for that . . ."

"*You have already given plenty . . . . It is now up to everyone to find out for himself or herself. You have to EXPERIENCE the Truth to say you know the Truth. You have to EXPERIENCE Spirit before you can say that you know Spirit. More words won't help.*"

"But just a few more chapters," I pleaded.

"*Tell them to read your book, one more time, and then again and again, and each time they will see more, discover more, and eventually they will be on the road of*"

more knowledge and insights. They will begin to experience life around them with new eyes and a new open
mind. They will begin to think with their hearts. This
experience will soon bring wisdom. That's how they will
learn."

"But to live and to experience life as it goes by
takes time, and a whole lifetime may go by before they
really learn."

"So? Time is a place. The past and the future belong to
the same room of time."

"What do you mean?"

"There is no time. There is only Eternity. Time is
what you make it to be. You can step into the "room of
time" and recreate what you call time."

"This is interesting. Can you explain more?"

"Explain more? You apply this principle every day in

your work. Of course, how would you know? And how would you remember?"

"I don't understand."

"When you step into the room of time you transform yourself into a higher frequency to make the transformation possible. You can do so only if you let go of any kind of human judgment. And when you are in that higher frequency, you have left your human brain behind, with all your human feelings, all logic, control and explanations . . . ."

"You mean one has to let go . . . totally . . . of thinking, comparing, trying to understand . . . Yes, I am good at that," I laughed. "I stopped thinking a long time ago, and now I just let go, and go with the flow. Yes, you're right, it does seem to work."

"To make a judgment is to stay in the limitation. Judgment is the obstacle separating you from the limitation and the Truth. And the ones who make the judgment

are the ones who often believe they know more, when usually the innocence of a child is closer to the Truth. When you know the Truth, you live the Truth genuinely and that way you manifest that you really do know!"

"I now make no judgments regarding limitations, what is possible and what is not possible, and through this I have found that I can be an instrument of the Light to do good for all people of all nations. Have I now arrived at the higher level?"

"Yes, you have, and no, you haven't. Once you are in the Light, there are still several levels inside of the Light. You still have to continue to go through one step after the other, although you are in the Light, to reach the Perfection. The Perfection is a never-ending continuation and not an end-station."

"Can you explain the Perfection more clearly?"

"I just sent you the answer to this, and you have accepted my answer on our level of oneness within you.

But you are unable to take my answer with you to the physical level of consciousness, where you now exist and where you have to explain it through a word. But you may call what is considered the Perfection: the 'Eternity, or the infinite zone of balance.' "

"And knowledge? What is knowledge?"

"Again, knowledge is never ending. You have reached the level of having knowledge when you are part of the knowledge and experience the knowledge first hand. When you have spiritual knowledge, the door of the Light will open up before you, and you can use the Light as your tool. You become part of the Oneness. You and I are then one."

"So why should I write this book at all when everything is supposed to be our own *experience*, and you have to live the knowledge to understand it?"

"Because classes, books, helping hands, and advice from others who are more knowledgeable are still Spirit's way to

offer knowledge on a level acceptable to everyone. There is a level for each one of us and you have the free will to continue as far as you feel the need for it. In the end, for the completion of knowledge you still have to LIVE it and walk the road on your own."

"Where do I personally fit in with all this?"

"You express this knowledge of being part of the Oneness in your healing sessions. Without you realizing it, you are working in the room of time. Intuitively you leave the dimension you like to call the NOW and step into the room of time. And there, in the dimension of the past, you discover the cause for the physical imbalance. You adjust the situation for the better and instants later, you step out of the room of time and return to your NOW. A healing has now taken place."

"Thank you for letting me know. You see, I had no idea this was how it worked!"

"How could you? You cannot prove how this is possi-

ble, because your physical brain, where your logic lives, is of a "slower" frequency than the level where you step in. There are no words, no magic formula to reach this level. This process is called "walking through the instant," and for you it is no process but a step. It is still a process of vast implications."

"Remember that when your physical body dies, your physical brain and all its education die with it. When you work with time, you have to go to the higher level, and bypass what you call brain to a level where you are in a direct connection with the Ultimate energy, with or without a working physical brain."

"I now understand how I can speak to those who are in a coma, seriously suffer from senility, or are even dead. You mean when I am one with you there are no more limitations regarding what is possible?"

"That's right. When you align with the Light, the I AM, the Me within, you will find unlimited possibilities. Only your humanity will make restrictions—what is possible or not possible."

"Why was I born?"

"*It was your wish to be born. You were born at a pre-destined time, into a predestined place, to parents and a situation you had chosen for yourself. Your higher self had a wish to be reborn for a good reason. But when you came into the physical body, you had forgotten about your reason to be born. You had also forgotten about your spiritual body. Instead, you learned to satisfy your new physical body and to do your best to keep it alive and well. Your basic reason to live on Earth is to learn how to experience the Oneness.*

Everyone is of the same Oneness, but through your choice of bodies and circumstances, you have chosen to separate yourselves not only from your origin but also from each other."

"You mean like Adam and Eve?"

"*Yes exactly like Adam and Eve. They were of the one and the same when they were in spirit. But when they were born into the physical, they found they had bodies, with many needs and a free will as well. That was when their problems began."*

"You make it sound so simple."

"It IS simple. Only your physical brains have made it so complicated."

"So what about women, and men and women."

"Yes, what about them?"

"Why am I a woman and not a man?"

"Because this was your choice. You came to this world to express womanhood and spirituality, and could only do so if you lived a life as a woman. Only women can truly experience what it means to be a woman. And feminine energy and spirituality are of the same energy frequency."

"So, are women and men really different?"

"In spirit you are both of the same oneness. In Spirit there is no difference, and there is no difference until you have found yourself a body. Men or women come out of the same pool, and in that pool there is only perfection. Perfection is never ending. In the perfection there is absolutely everything. From the perfection you unconditionally chose your body, as well as your blueprint of tasks and memories and what talent you would like to use.

Through your choices you created lessons for you to learn, either in the body of a man or in the body of a woman. Or as a Muslim, Jew, Hindu, or Christian, black or white, yellow, blue or green. Only that way will you learn the perfection. Sometimes you are born rich. Other times what you may call poor. And in the end you are to decide what is really rich and what is really poor. At the time when you made your choice, you knew and understood the reason for your choices. You then chose a body and a life, and you made this choice unconditionally and out of the highest love. Therefore, no conception is by chance or a mistake. It was always meant to be."

"And what about you? Why do we think of you as a man?"

"Because this is the way your civilizations have chosen it to be. You must realize that when you call me "He," you exclude much of the energy called "Everything" from your sub-conscience, and this limitation is the reason why my greatness is not fully understood."

"I know, and when I first heard your voice, I thought I heard a man, because I'd been told you were a "man." Once I got to know you better, and understood how absolutely immeasurable you are, the voice I now hear is a man-woman-and-it-all, a voice of all dimensions. And you speak all the five languages I know at the same time, and I still very clearly hear everything you say! I have begun to understand your greatness, and how we humans have set a limit to who you are and to what we are. Unfortunately, limitation is all we have allowed ourselves to accept."

I could've continued my conversation with Spirit, but I felt I'd absorbed as much as possible for a while. As I left the beach, I watched an elderly couple sit down on the sand not far from me. They were holding hands and looked relaxed and happy together. I was so absorbed by the moment of my connection with the Oneness, that I unintentionally tuned in to their energies. Yes, they were happy, but their life together had not been easy. They'd had many financial challenges, and a separation after the death of their child. But they'd soon made peace with their loss and then started all over again. Now, they had learned to free themselves of the past and to enjoy the little things in their lives. To intentionally connect with Spirit had never been a priority in their life, but in many ways they'd already done so through their positive outlook, and the contentment they now experienced.

A few days later, on a regular Wednesday afternoon, I was home alone, preparing myself for several telephone consultations. I liked working over the telephone to help people find their life's direction or to feel better physically. It seemed to work very well.

Although I never met the person before, I could still see his or her energy-field in front of me and forgot there were sometimes thousands of miles and several continents between us. But it really didn't matter, because I'd found that one can project Light and positive energy to a recipient, no matter how far away they were, and through this energy help and healing would occur, and new, positive energies would be created. In fact it would often work better over the telephone because people would stay in the comfort of their homes instead of being distracted by bus schedules, parking meters or concerns that they had to rush back to work immediately afterwards.

As I sat by the window in my library, with the dogs sleeping beside me on the floor, the room suddenly appeared so white and bright, and a feeling of complete calm arose around me. I looked up.

We had met before: But this time, He was all in white. His robe, His appearance—everything was white. In His hands he carried what looked like a very healthy, green palm leaf, and He handed it towards me. He was not as close to me this time as before, and I didn't feel his energy the same way. But his presence made me feel extremely peaceful and calm. Like I had done something right and that I now had come home.

I never heard a voice, but his words were still so clear. He said we like to call him Jesus:

"I AM . . . *IS* . . . the Light within you. Your Light within you is the accumulation of All and Everything of the Universe within each one of you. The more you focus on the Light within you, the more powerful your I AM within you will be."

I knew. It sounded like a reminder of the first commandment. But I was confused. I needed to know more.

It sounded like a philosophy we all know—but seen and interpreted a different way. This way it appeared so simple, so loving, and including all of us.

"Why me?" I asked Him through my heart. It was the same question I'd asked so many times for so many years. "Why do you come to *me*?"

"Because you set no limits to what is. You are always open and willing to know more."

I had one more question I felt it was necessary to ask, but I hesitated. It was a sensitive subject. And, as if He'd heard my question, He continued:

"I am also Me—the Person, the Word, the Idea. I am the accumulation of your thoughts and many prayers. Your spoken words have created me, the person you wish me to be, and the more you send to me of your love and prayers, the stronger I, and my energy, will become."

Then he disappeared. It seemed as though he'd stayed for a long, long time. Yes, he'd answered my questions. I now felt that I *knew*. I knew in my soul, I knew in my heart, I knew in my head.

Should I tell others?

I did.

Did it make any difference in their lives?

I don't think so.

Why?

To understand, we must first go through our own experiences. Then we make choices. Nobody else can go through your experiences for you. Nor can others make your choices for you. Nobody else can change your mindset and belief, if you don't want to do so.

Did this experience make a difference in my life?

Yes, an incredible difference. So many of my thoughts had been answered. About religion in general, about Christianity in particular. My faith in Spirit as non-denominational strengthened and I'd experienced first hand how all faiths belong to an incredible Universal Oneness of energy, where everyone plays a role trying to be in harmony. All of us live in a limitless Universe, where each one of us is part of this Oneness. Each one of us shines, and everyone has a chance to create their own reality.

Again, I had gone through yet one more awakening.

This is what life is all about: As energy beings we are meant to keep on opening doors, to reach new levels and to be part of a continuum of Oneness. To do so, we go through never-ending awakenings: One after the other, throughout our lifetime, the awakenings will never cease. Because the knowledge of which we are a part is never ending.

A few weeks later, as I was cleaning out some old financial files from my filing cabinet, I came across a yellow notepaper that didn't seem to belong among the others. Flabbergasted, I read the handwritten lines. And my thoughts went back to a lovely weekend in the beginning of May ten years earlier almost to the day, when I was staying with good friends for a few relaxing days in the Rocky Mountains. As so often was my habit, I had gone for a short hike by myself in the early morning. It was a crisp, beautiful morning and I'd brought some fruit and a writing pad along. I'd planned to take a break, and in peace and quiet prepare for an upcoming charity committee meeting in Florida. At that time I was still married to Jack and busy with my many charity events.

Imagine my surprise when I later discovered that instead of writing a draft for a committee agenda, I suddenly found that my hand was writing on my pad at full speed and without any intervention from my side. Amazed, I found myself making periods and capital letters for new sentences, and then, almost magically, the writing stopped.

"What on earth is *THIS?*" I burst out, and was even more amazed as I casually read through what had been written. I had expected only senseless scribbles of words. But, with a shiver, and shaking my head in disbelief, I found "I" had written two pages of numbered guidelines. They were for me, and although they made perfect sense, I couldn't see how they would fit into my life. The list eventually disappeared out of my sight, and I forgot all about it.

But now, I was flabbergasted. When I read the handwritten note with the guidelines I previously had been so mystified by, they now suddenly made perfect sense. In fact, they were the rules I now unknowingly lived by. It appeared that not only had I received them in writing, they had at the same time been planted in my heart. They had been guiding me all along. To find this piece of paper was a confirmation that I was on the right road, and that there *IS* a plan for each one of us. Of course, it's up to each one of us to accept it or reject it.

Most of all: It was a reminder that we are never alone.

These are the instructions I was given. For me they were a message spoken directly from Spirit.

But this message is for you too. Because we all belong to the same universal Oneness, where each one of us has been given our own connection to Spirit with a God-given sparkle within us with the potential to be our own leader in how we are to conduct our lives.

1.

YOU ARE ONE WITH THE UNIVERSAL ENERGY AND
YOU ARE TO CONNECT WITH IT DAILY.

2.

LISTEN TO YOUR INNER VOICE.
THIS IS HOW I SPEAK TO YOU.

3.

BE WITH THOSE WHO HAVE A POSITIVE
OUTLOOK AND WHO MAKE YOU
FEEL GOOD. THIS WAY YOU WILL FIND MORE
INSPIRATION, POWER AND HAPPINESS.

4.

BE OPEN AND SEE BEYOND
YOUR OWN HORIZON.
THIS IS HOW YOU WILL FIND MORE
KNOWLEDGE AND HOW YOUR
LESSONS WILL BE LEARNED.

5.

MY FRIENDS ARE YOUR FRIENDS. WE ARE
EVERYWHERE AND YOU ARE TO FIND
STRENGTH IN US.

6.

DO NOT ALLOW SICKNESS, ENVY,
BITTERNESS, GREED OR CONDITIONAL LOVE TO
CONTROL YOUR LIFE
THIS WILL WEAKEN YOU.

7.

YOU CAN DO WHAT YOU WISH TO DO,
AND WHAT YOU WISH TO DO IS IN
YOUR HEART.

8.

YOU WILL REACH TRUE KNOWLEDGE,
HAPPINESS AND SUCCESS
THROUGH YOUR OWN AWAKENINGS.

9.

IT IS UP TO YOU TO BE YOUR OWN
SUCCESS LEADER.

10.

YOU AND I ARE ONE.
THIS IS YOUR FIRST AND LAST
COMMANDMENT.

There is a divine plan for each one of us—no matter who we are and where we live. Once we have connected with the energy of our divine plan, and can experience first hand the feeling of being one with the whole universe, we'll begin to walk a road of many awakenings. And as we do, we'll find that we see more, hear more and understand more. We'll become more tolerant and unconditionally loving. We now grow both emotionally and spiritually. Invisible walls that had previously set a limit to what we had decided we could believe in have now disappeared and a new reality without limitations to what we truly are, is opening up before us.

Not until now do we comprehend what it really means to be rich. To have riches is not the amount of money that we have accumulated in a worldly bank account. To be rich is to know how to access the abundance of knowledge that already exists within you. This wealth is YOURS and it is absolutely unlimited.

Nobody can ever take that away from you.

Epilogue

"Mom!" I immediately recognized the frantic tone of my daughter's voice on the other end of the telephone. "Dad is sick. I'm with him in the hospital, and he wants you to come and see him—right now."

I hesitated, but said nothing. I knew Jack's health had been failing for some time, but we hadn't been in touch since our divorce several years earlier. It now seemed almost surprising that he suddenly wanted to see me again.

"Please, please do come," Annabel continued, quite upset. "I don't know if he is going to live much longer, and he really wants to see you . . . ," my daughter insisted.

So often since our divorce I'd wanted to see Jack again, remain friends, be together for a few hours with our daughter and granddaughter, and laugh like old times. There was no doubt in my mind that once we were meant to be together, and I was troubled by the fact that we'd never had the proper closure to our marriage; a conclusion that our signatures on all the legal documents had been unable to offer. Jack had always refused to meet again, and as I became increasingly occupied with my work, the years quickly passed by. And now, all of a sudden, Jack had finally found the emotional freedom to change his mind.

"If you don't get together now, I'll never have peace in my heart. And nor will the two of you," Annabel proceeded, as if she had read my mind.

"And if you and dad won't have peace in your hearts, we'll all have to be reincarnated into the same situation—not only you and dad, but me too!"

Annabel paused for a few moments, then she added: "I don't think I want to go through this lifetime one more time. So you'd better come here before it's too late. He so much wants to talk to you."

I was proud of Annabel, speaking for her father, with whom she had remained very close through the years. But most of all I was proud because she so early in life had understood that our lives are about giving, forgiving, letting go and maybe starting all over again.

Of course, I wanted to see Jack again. I had hoped for this moment for years.

As I sat down by Jack's bedside, it seemed as though we had never been separated at all. Gone were all the memories of dispute or bitterness. Back were the times when we enjoyed being together. We held each other's hands, saying nice things to each other. Jack didn't look sick, but he appeared . . . so defeated.

It was painful to see this formerly so impressive man look that way.

"I missed you," I said and held his hand. I really meant it. I had missed our good times.

"I missed you too," Jack answered. He hadn't noticed my concern for his looks. "I missed you very much," he added and closed his eyes. The medication had made him drowsy and at times he had trouble keeping his eyes open.

Annabel left us alone for a while, as Jack and I talked about old times. We had a long marriage behind us and it seemed so natural to hold hands again. He asked about my family and all the friends we used to have in common. And he said he loved me. He appeared more and more peaceful as the hours went by.

I wondered why we'd never sat down like that before we had decided on a divorce. Things might have been very different if we had. Jack knew about my doctorate and seemed proud, although he didn't seem to understand my new profession.

Jack had gone to Jesuit School and often mentioned his Catholic background. But somehow he was superstitious about Spirit and death, and I recalled how he had told me many years earlier that when he died, he wanted "a hell of a good Catholic preacher" for his funeral service, to secure his entrance to Heaven.

When I finally said my goodbyes to Jack, it was probably the hardest goodbye of my life. Although I didn't perceive any of the yellow-grayish death-rays I usually see around those who are about to pass over, I knew I would never see him again. But I felt deep down in my heart that we had reached a complete and beautiful closure.

When we kissed a final good-bye, I knew I also said goodbye to a whole lifetime, where all the pain and hurt were not only forgiven but also completely forgotten. We were both friends again. The cycle was completed—for both of us.

With tears filling my eyes, I finally left the hospital. It was now late in the evening and the hospital night guards were already patrolling the parking lot. I picked a white flower from the planter by the hospital entrance and slowly went to my car with the little flower in my hand. In spirit, the little flower was meant for Jack.

As in a trance, with tears rolling down over my face, I drove along the ocean heading back to my home in Miami Beach. It was a clear night, and there were hardly any other cars on the road that ran through the narrow stretch of land separating the ocean beaches from the calm waters of the Intracoastal Waterway.

Suddenly I was startled: they played "our" song on the car radio. The song that Jack and I had enjoyed and danced to during our honeymoon and always cherished through the years.

The sound of the music awakened me from my numbness, and I realized I had just passed by the spot alongside the road, where Jack and I had made a short stop the day of our first date to watch some fishermen pull fish out of the water. We were on our way from Miami to have lunch in Fort Lauderdale, about one-hour drive north of Miami.

At that moment, I happened to look at the dashboard, and I was so amazed that I had to stop the car. I was confused. Almost trembling, I reached for the daily newspaper lying beside me on the front seat to confirm the day and the date: What I saw was true, and I was totally speechless.

My God!

It couldn't be.

But it was!

Because not only had Jack and I driven on that same road between Miami Beach and Fort Lauderdale, and stopped exactly at that particular place, when "our" song suddenly aired over the car radio, we had done so at that exact same minute, and on that very same day and date! I still remembered everything about that day, and how I had asked Jack for the time at that particular place.

Now, so many years later, I was driving back on that same road, exactly at the same hour, the same date, at the same place as the radio was playing our song.

This was too much to be a mere coincidence.

But this time it wasn't early in the day. The time

was not five minutes before 12 noon as it was before, when we drove north on the same road. Instead, it was five minutes before 12—shortly before midnight. But I was driving alone now, and going back south, back to where we had started, many years before.

In the eyes of the universe, our life together had been nothing but a 12-hour day. That day was now definitely over and I had been given the sign that the day had been brought to completion.

For me, it had been the longest of days. But in the room of time, our long day together would just leave a little glimmer of energy, luckily an energy that had now been transformed into a positive and loving one.

Yet one more time, I had learned: We have been born to be part of a particular universal plan, and within that plan, there are even more plans. These plans come our way in the form of what we believe to be coincidences, or synchronicity. But there are no coincidences, only offers and possibilities to do things a certain way.

When we are aware, we notice. There is so much "out there" for all of us to use and take advantage of.

So many ways to enjoy life and to make not only our own existence but also the whole world a better place.

It is up to us, each one of us, to recognize that Everything is out there for us. All we have to do is to be in tune.

Everyone who is seriously involved in the pursuit

of science becomes convinced that a Spirit

is manifest in the Laws of the Universe.

— *Albert Einstein*

Acknowledgments

I recognize in gratitude that my work has been made possible by the continuous and loving persistence of Spirit and will forever remain grateful for the many new and exciting possibilities that have incessantly opened up before me. Usually when I least expected it, always reassuring me of the true purpose of my life. I am also grateful that my life has been touched by so many wonderful and well meaning people, who believed in my vision and were there to support me in my endeavors. "Without your helping hands it would not have been possible for me to reach out to so many and be where I am now."

To my beautiful daughter Annika and my lovely grandchildren Arianna and Mattias, thank you for your incredible spiritual awareness and for always being there for me.

Thank you to my friends Wildfrid de Flon, Gunilla von Post and Sharon Hamilton for always lending me an ear and for your support and friendship at all times.

Last but not least for helping me put this book together I would like to extend my sincere thank you to Nina L. Diamond, Christine DeLorey, Margaret Copeland, Ken Peterson, Dan Danielson and Susan Hicks. You were a great team.

About the Author

HELENA STEINER-HORNSTEYN, a native of Sweden, was born with the gift to intuitively see energy-fields inside and around the human body. With time she discovered that all of us have certain cellular memory cells within the body that contain the *actual cause* for physical and emotional imbalance and that this information could be changed—intuitively, so people got well. She is ranked one of the top four in the world in the field of intuitive healing and spiritual development, and works on the principle that we are energy, everything around us is energy and that energy never dies. She holds a Doctorate of Divinity degree and maintains medical intuitive offices in both the United States and in Europe.

Before her spiritual calling, Dr. Helena was active in the international business world, was a busy socialite and a world traveler. But her many extraordinary spiritual experiences finally came to completely change the future of her life.

She was the Founder and former Chairman of the Institute for Positive Living in Berlin and Baden-Baden, Germany, and the Founder and Chairman of the Symphony Guild of South Florida, a not for profit organization that has provided scholarships for exceptional music students and promoted international cultural exchange programs. She also founded and supported two South Florida Symphony orchestras, to mention just a few of her charitable activities.

She is a mother and grandmother, and lectures in the U.S and internationally, dividing her time between her medical intuitive practices in Europe and in the U.S. Helena now lives in South Florida.

This book is meant to be read again and again.

Each time you'll see the Truth a different way.

ACTIVALE Institute

A Global Enterprise for Human Development and World Peace

P.O. Box 315
Sarasota, FL 34270

For books, meditation CDs, one-on-ones, lectures and workshops
go to www.ACTIVALE.com
Email: activale@aol.com or activale@gmail.com

Understand the Magic of

Your True Self.

Begin to unfold

And discover the Truth

About Yourself.

CPSIA information can be obtained at www.ICGtesting.com
Printed in the USA
LVOW12s0459200116

471114LV00001B/1/P